TWYLA THARP

Keep It Moving

Lessons for the Rest of Your Life

Simon & Schuster

NEW YORK   LONDON   TORONTO   SYDNEY   NEW DELHI

Simon & Schuster
1230 Avenue of the Americas
New York, NY 10020

First Simon & Schuster hardcover edition October 2019

SIMON & SCHUSTER and colophon are registered trademarks of Simon & Schuster, Inc.

For information about special discounts for bulk purchases, please contact
Simon & Schuster Special Sales at 1-866-506-1949 or business@simonandschuster.com.

The Simon & Schuster Speakers Bureau can bring authors to your live event.
For more information or to book an event, contact the Simon & Schuster Speakers
Bureau at 1-866-248-3049 or visit our website at www.simonspeakers.com.

Interior design by Paul Dippolito

Manufactured in the United States of America

10   9   8   7   6   5   4   3   2   1

Library of Congress Cataloging-in-Publication Data

Names: Tharp, Twyla, author.
Title: Keep it moving : lessons for the rest of your life / Twyla Tharp.
Description: New York : Simon & Schuster, 2019. | Summary: "One of the world's leading
    artists—a living legend—and bestselling author of The Creative Habit shares her
    secrets for harnessing vitality and finding purpose as you age. From insight to action,
    Keep It Moving is a   guidebook for expanding one's possibilities over the course of a
    lifetime"—Provided by publisher.
Identifiers: LCCN 2019025680 (print) | LCCN 2019025681 (ebook) | ISBN 9781982101305
    (hardcover) | ISBN 9781982101312 (paperback) | ISBN 9781982101329 (ebook)
Subjects: LCSH: Self-actualization (Psychology) | Older people--Psychology. Meaning
    (Psychology) | Aging
Classification: LCC BF637.S4 T43 2019 (print) | LCC BF637.S4 (ebook) |
    DDC 158.1--dc23
LC record available at https://lccn.loc.gov/2019025680
LC ebook record available at https://lccn.loc.gov/2019025681

ISBN 978-1-9821-0130-5
ISBN 978-1-9821-0132-9 (ebook)

This book is for my grandson, Teph,
and his wonderful parents,
Jesse and Lea.

CONTENTS

Keep It Moving

Chapter 1

Terms and Conditions

Twenty years ago, I wrote a book called *The Creative Habit*, sharing the message that we can all live creative lives if only we could stop waiting for a muse to arrive with divine inspiration and instead just get down to work. In other words, you too can be more creative if you are willing to sweat a little. This message still resonates when I lecture. But, interestingly, the question I am most often asked after a talk these days is on a different topic entirely: "How do you keep working?" The subtext here, *sotto voce*, is ". . . at your age?" Which is seventy-eight.

To me it is simple. I continue to work as I always have, expecting each day to build on the one before. And I do not see why I should not continue to work in this spirit.

Keep It Moving is intended to encourage those who wish to maintain their prime a very long time. Like most books of practical advice, it identifies a "disease" and offers a cure. That disease, simply put, is our fear of time passing and the resulting aging process. The remedy? The book in your hands.

I flirted with the idea of calling this book *The Youth Habit*. I liked the suggestion that youth's virtues could be easily transplanted into our post-youth years if only we followed a routine: take the stairs, use sunscreen, ingest more omega-3s and fewer omega-6s, don't shortchange yourself on sleep. Cut out sugar, do something nice for someone else daily, floss, read more, watch less, love the one you're with, and it's okay to drink wine (until the next study says it isn't). Sounded like a bestseller to me.

But if experience has taught me anything, it's that chasing youth is a losing proposition. There's little benefit in looking back, at least not with yearning or nostalgia or any other melancholy humor. To look back is to cling to something well over and behind you. We don't lose youth. Youth stays put. We move on. We need to face the fact that aging will happen to us along with everybody else and just get on with it. Growing older is a strange stew of hope, despair, courage—still I think you will agree—it is light-years ahead of the alternative.

I don't promise eternal youth in *Keep It Moving*. I have no interest in sugarcoating the aging process. What I believe in is change and the vitality it brings. Vitality means moving through life with energy and vigor, making deliberate choices and putting to good use the time and energy that we have been granted. You have, no doubt, seen people in their late seventies or even into their nineties who don't seem worn out by their years but instead welcome the opportunity to be truly present in their bodies and in their minds. Instead of stubbornly staying on known paths, afraid to stray, they look at what comes next with curiosity, expanding into whatever it may be.

So, no, this book is not *The Youth Habit*. Nor is it *The Creative Habit*—which promotes regularity in living and working—because as we grow older, it is just as important to break habits as it is to make them.

I want to reprogram how you think about aging by getting rid of two corrosive ideas. First, that you need to emulate youth, resolving to live in a corner of the denial closet marked "reserved for aged." Second, that your life must contract with time. Let's start by breaking some old thought patterns.

I've danced my entire life (and still do) and I've spent time with many great performers. For these dancers and athletes, the passage of time presents mostly difficult realities. The jump declines, speed diminishes, flexibility is challenged. And fear of decline and irrelevance starts early.

Years ago, I was sitting in a coffee shop with a dancer of remarkable talents, Mikhail Baryshnikov. We had just finished one of the early rehearsals for *Push Comes to Shove*, a ballet I wrote for him. Even then it was clear that he was a phenomenon, one of the very greatest classical dancers of the twentieth century. Though he was in his prime, he was looking morose as we drank our coffee. I asked him, "Misha, what's the matter? You don't like what we're doing?" No, he said, he loved what we were doing; "But," he added, "soon we will be old." He was all of twenty-seven. And yet I understood.

For dancers, aging is ever in front of us as we work. We face it each time we enter the studio, one day older than the day before. But who among us in the civilian population has not shared the feeling that they, too, will be finished by forty? It needles when things don't work the way they used to. And it doesn't help that, gradually, as joints begin to ache and memory to slip, we are bombarded by negative messages from our culture. Older adults are frequently portrayed as out of touch, useless, feeble, incompetent, pitiful, and irrelevant. Sadly, these dismal expectations can become self-fulfilling, creating the bias that fuels our roaring age industry—pills, diets, special cosmetics, surgery—all promising to send time reeling backward. But no. Time goes only one way: forward.

The result? Frustration becomes a habit. Little indignities become a reason to rant and complain. But that scenario will bleed out your spirit, take away your resiliencies. If you go into situations always expecting to be cheated or deprived, you'll likely find ways to tell yourself that is exactly what has happened. Don't go searching for things that confirm or fuel your sense of indignation. It will become a default mind-set promoting more of the same.

Let's agree:

Age is not the enemy. Stagnation is the enemy. Complacency is the enemy. Stasis is the enemy. Attempting to maintain the status quo, smoothing our skin, and keeping our tummies trim become distractions that obscure a larger truth. Attempting to freeze your life in time at any point is totally destructive to the prospect of a life lived well and fully. All animate creatures are destroyed when frozen. They do not move. This is not a worthy goal.

However, the forces that create inertia in our lives are difficult to resist for they are hardwired into us. People prefer to keep going along as they always have rather than make a decision that would knock them out of their groove, even when it would be relatively easy to change course. Behavioral scientists refer to this as *status quo bias*. We succumb to this bias with habits large and small, from an inability to give up our three cups of coffee a day to staying with a partner long after it's clear that the relationship is over. The devil best known becomes our buddy.

Along with status quo bias, there is another habit I'd like to undo. As we get older and our bodies enjoy less natural freedom of movement, we tend to take up less space, both physically and metaphorically. Here's the end-point of this tendency: our backs arch forward, no longer straight and long. Our steps shorten from a stride to a shuffle. Our vision narrows, slowly erasing the periphery, leaving only what's in front of our nose. No wonder we prefer remaining at home, our life lived in fewer and fewer rooms. We let our bodies constrict, inviting the world around us to close in.

The mind will follow the body's contraction. On this path, our concerns narrow down to the most elemental functions: what to eat, getting enough sleep, keeping an appointment.

Contraction is not inevitable. You can resist and reverse.

Now to form some new habits. I hope in these pages to get you to wake up and move more. After all, I repeat, to move is the provenance of all living human beings. And by my definition, to move is to dance. With the time you've got, choose to make your life bigger. Opt for expression over observation, action instead of passivity, risk over safety, the unknown over the familiar. Be deliberate, act with intention. Chase the sublime and the absurd. Make each day one where you emerge, unlock, excite, and discover. Find new, reconsider old, become limber, stretch, lean, move . . . I say this with love: shut up and dance. That was the advice I gave myself for my sixty-fifth birthday. You might want to start now.

I will try to help. Each chapter includes an approach to moving that can be practiced by the beginner as well as the advanced. These exercises are reflective of simple actions we all use every day. Begin now.

TAKE UP SPACE

When your muscles stretch rather than constrict, you expand your share of the planet. You take up more space, not less. Dancers know this intuitively. They are taught to move so that every gesture is not only more precise and elegant but bigger. We call it *amplitude.* It is not enough to state an arabesque; it must be opened in every direction to its full expanse. In order to be seen, the dancer must occupy maximum volume. You can think the same way in your everyday movements.

- When you walk, think of yourself striding, not just taking mingy steps.
- Greeting a friend, reach your arm out, whether to shake a hand or give a hug, with amplitude and full fellow feeling. Be robust.
- During a meeting, spread your belongings out across the table instead of gathering them tidily in your lap. Speak out. Take up mental space as well.

There is logic in our movement. Remember, when we walk, we go forward. We can move backward, but we are not designed for this. Forward is our natural way.

Think of this all as your personal Occupy More Space protest.

With this in mind, consider what would happen if you continued to conduct your life beyond forty-five to arrive at seventy-five as a powerful beginning point, where, honed and strengthened by experience, you could use a lifetime's efforts to give yourself new options in both how you address work and how you live with those you love. Why not insist on continuing to make fundamental choices for yourself, not leaving it to chance and "how things will be"? Why not evaluate your accomplishments as beginnings rather than endings.

Amass the experiences and grow into the person you were meant to be. One of the first lessons in the studio is that if you want to be something, you've got to train to be it over and over. Master cellist Pablo Casals was asked late in life, "Why practice at age ninety-one?" "Because I am making progress" was his answer. Right!

Practice growth. This is one habit I encourage you to cultivate. What you do today is an investment in tomorrow. With that in mind, to the list of desirable states of emotional equilibrium that end in "-ness"—for example, wellness, mindfulness, forgiveness, friendliness, decisiveness, hopefulness, and the really big one, happiness—let me add a personal favorite: *expansiveness*. Moving out is moving on, time and space working in tandem. Expansiveness is a factor of the following four ingredients:

1. Intention is the umbrella term for our desires, ambitions, and designs for the future. Intention defines our next move, and the next, and the one after that. It's how we plan and control our life. Without it, we're either marching in place or losing ground.

2. Honest appraisal of the past is how we deal with the inevitable setbacks, failures, and embarrassments life hands us. Without it, we cannot self-correct or recover. We will be forever mired in regret and guilt, wanting to change what we've already done to create a new outcome. Only happens in science fiction.

3. Anger about the past is the killer emotion. It's noise not signal. Crank it up to high volume and it cancels out the sound of our best intentions.

4. Energy and time are self-explanatory, but as tools they are force multipliers. If you have an abundance of time and energy but waste it by getting stuck in the stale routines of the past, you have no chance of moving forward.

If we can husband and direct our time and energy, the quality of each day or year will spring from a marriage of intention and disciplined effort rather than a reliance on luck or genetic birthright. We make a choice. We invest our time and energy. We reap the reward or take the hit. Whatever the result, we are constantly working on what comes next. We earn our life.

Make a contract with your future. Facing new habits requires accountability. Here are the terms and conditions of our agreement:

- Acknowledge you have choices. Make them.

- Your body will be a big part of this deal and you will be ready and able to use it.

- You will be okay to reidentify yourself often along the way.

- Obstacles—you will meet many—go around, over, under, or through. Again often.

- Bounce back—yes, many, many times.

- Up is preferred to down.

- Stamina is your bailiwick. Train. Train more.

- Bend in the wind.

- Get stronger for the mending.

- Dance is being in motion. You are doing it. Do it more.

What I want us to do is abandon our infatuation with the status quo and jettison our aversion to every form of risk, acknowledge we are getting older; pledge to get over it and get moving.

That's the deal. Turn the page.

Chapter Two

The Life
We Choose

Exercise 2: Practice Pushing Back *page 22*

I chose my life, it did not choose me.

I remember the moment. November 1962. I was in a dressing room between dance classes. I was twenty-one. It was seven months before my college graduation, and I was thinking about the future.

What are you going to do? I kept asking myself.

Dance, came the response. Gut-level reflex, but not so simple.

I'd been studying art history. It would have made more sense for me to pursue a career in that field. At least it was a clear course of action. About dancing, I knew nothing except dancers made little money and had a very short career span. However, when I made my choice, I thought about what I cared for most. Art history might have had weekly paychecks, but I did not see it as my destiny.

Clearly, I'd had some inkling that dance would be my life at least a year earlier when I'd transferred from college in California to Manhattan in order to be at the center of the dance world. While I'd convinced my college administrators to let me pursue an independent study program shuttling between two disciplines—weekdays for dancing off-campus, weekends for cramming art history textbooks—I knew the student's life in dance I'd been practicing was different from a professional career. Mondays through Fridays, I'd grab my dance bag and find a class in one of Manhattan's many studios. I assessed the other dancers in class—many of them in-demand professionals. I felt good about my prospects. The women were strong and fast, but not patently stronger or faster than I. They had polish and finesse, but I could acquire those qualities with more work.

Okay, I can do this, I thought. *There's a life here.*

It was a decision to set off in my own direction and see where it led. I left the dressing room decided.

That was the beginning of my pledge. In the Old French, *pleige* means the security or bail that released a hostage. Our pledges can help free us from the indecision that holds us hostage, a prisoner of inaction. When you think of a pledge, you might think of a promise made at the beginning of a new venture, but I suggest an alternate understanding.

To me, a pledge is revealed over time, like a Polaroid picture coming into focus. The moments when you make choices—move across country for a job or stay in your hometown, have another child or don't, phone a friend in need or give them space—come together in a constellation that maps what matters to you most.

I promised I would not try to convince you that aging is a gift, but that does not mean we can't find benefits in getting older. One of these is that you can step back from your life to see its whole shape. A pledge comes into clearer focus over the course of your life—it shows itself not rigid but bending with a momentum powerful enough to dictate what the next day will be.

You determine your pledge through your choices.

You have probably grappled with a barrage of choices in one way or another over the years. You are offered a job, but the hours are abominable. You get back worrisome test results from your physician. You feel a calling to investigate a field unrelated to the career you've pursued for decades. What are you going to do?

There is no surefire way to make a correct choice, but I offer this: the only choice that is certain to be wrong is the one you don't make. Eliminate inaction as a choice. Your bigger, freer, better life starts with a choice to act.

While it is true that some choices are best made with slow deliberation, grave thought given to the consequences and responsibilities of our actions, other choices, in situations equally intense, are made with great speed by the body, its thinking unbidden by the mind. At moments of extreme emotion we do not tell the body what to do. We fall in love: boom. A ten-ton truck headed directly for us: we swerve. Death of a loved one: instant profound sadness. These choices our bodies make untutored by the mind.

The inevitable effect of time and trauma will dull these quick, gut-level choices. But too much thinking and fear of failure in advance will cause us to question every aspect involved in our decision-making, freezing us in our tracks. Not good.

The best choices are made instinctively. Bit by bit, these choices fill out your character over the course of a lifetime. Your pledge materializes out of observing the choices you make.

Our culture tells us that to feel rewarded, we must accomplish, achieve, check goals off a list. But a pledge is not a goal. A goal is a desire you articulate to yourself that has an endpoint. You want to be famous, or president, or retired at forty. You want to find a mate or speak Italian or fit into a size two. While pursuing a goal is admirable, I want to emphasize that a pledge is not a goal.

Take Diana Nyad, a champion long-distance swimmer. Over the course of thirty-five years, she had attempted the swim between Cuba and Florida four times, and each time had to make the prudent call to quit lest she risk death. In her quest to become the first person to swim this distance without the protection of a shark cage, Diana Nyad had encountered obstacles most of us never face, including poisonous box jellyfish and sharks. What she found as she entered her sixties, however, is all too familiar to most of us—a sense that she was on the sidelines of the life she was meant to lead. This was literally the case for her, as a sports broadcaster. As she writes, "I was a bystander, witnessing other people chasing their dreams. I was telling other people's stories instead of living out my own story. I was no longer a dreamer myself. I was no longer a doer."

After the death of her mother, she confronted her fear that she was wasting, as she quotes poet Mary Oliver, her one "wild and precious life," and she decided to attempt the swim that had defeated her four times as a much younger woman. Through rigorous training, careful planning, and unwavering determination, she became, at age sixty-four, the first person to make the 110-mile swim. Yes, she achieved her goal. Job well done. But as impressive as this pursuit was, it was a goal, not a pledge.

If you can mark it as "done," it's a goal. Not so with a pledge. Whatever you decide to pledge, it is essential that you are striving to reach it, always trying to refine, hone, and improve your choices to better fulfill it. Your pledge becomes a distillation of your life's work in action. You don't want to get to a point where you feel you are finished. Remember, when we are frozen, we are dead.

My pledge is a daily choice. We all see the distinction between a chosen life and an unintentional life when we apply it to other people. It's why we admire the self-made individual and resent the heir. The former satisfies our sense of equity; the latter offends it (why him, not me?).

Know what you want to do and do it. It is how I measure my work at each day's end: How well did I marry what I wanted to do and what I actually did? If I'm satisfied with the answer, I've chosen the day. Anything less is not a good feeling. The life we choose pays dividends. The life that we let choose us will bankrupt us.

Four months after college graduation, my pledge was beginning to unfold: I was dancing in a professional company. It was exhilarating, but I was restless and something didn't feel right. I began to audition for other jobs. I went in for the Radio City Rockettes, did a series of difficult moves well enough to be brought forward and told, "Young lady, you dance very well. But could you smile?"

I walked out.

"Now what are you going to do?" I asked myself.

I had chosen a physical life, but when I walked out of that audition, I realized that simply being a dancer, taking direction from others, couldn't fulfill me. If I wanted to dance, I would have to make the dances myself—become performer and choreographer, which is neither an obvious nor an enviable career progression. Of the thousands of ballerinas and hoofers and street dancers in the U.S., only a tiny handful become choreographers. I had no clue what the job meant. What I did know was that when I made up my own steps and when I hit movement that felt right, BINGO!

I should have been worried about my next meal, next class, next paycheck. But I took a longer view of my situation.

What I have learned throughout my life is to try to expand my opportunities rather than limit them, even when faced with an obstacle. What it came down to with me and the Rockettes was my unwillingness to join the line. The line is where you lose your identity and your independence.

So I became a choreographer. The first thing Greek playwrights undertook with new plays was to become their own choreographers, training the chorus to move. Before the music, and before the words, was the action. Choreography is literally to write action for a group: *choreo*—chorus; *graphy*—to write.

T his is how I would have you write your life: in action. It is not enough to intend or consider, you must choose to act, often and ongoingly. If dancing meant having to make the dances, so be it. Many carry the misconception that we should become more comfortable and that things should become easier as time goes by. This is a belief system designed to undermine you. In life, there will be problems. This is guaranteed. We must learn to use our obstacles, transforming them into advantages.

Karen von Blixen found herself in midlife facing loss on a monumental scale. In 1914 she had moved with her husband from Denmark to Kenya to set up a coffee plantation. She grew to love the farm, but her marriage did not fare well. Bror von Blixen was unfaithful, and Karen was diagnosed with syphilis, plagued with physical suffering for years. When the von Blixens divorced, Karen was left to manage the failing coffee business. Despite her best efforts, the farm went belly-up. Her next love, the adventurer Denys Finch Hatton, was killed in a plane crash—with another woman by his side. Karen returned to her family home in Denmark in 1931, brokenhearted and nearly penniless.

Failure, tragedy, financial ruin, emotional devastation. The only thing Karen hadn't lost was her mettle—and her talent. She had published minor works many years before, but it was only upon returning home from Kenya that she began to write in earnest. However she had actually been writing all along. She was writing letters. She was telling stories. She had memorized *The Arabian Nights*. She knew the Bible from cover to cover, absorbed its rhythms, and its cadences. In Africa what she had lacked was a necessity for writing, and that necessity came when there was nothing else she could do. When her life fell apart she found what she knew best was writing. And so she turned to it, finally.

Her commitment—made halfway through her life—to writing was a courageous redirection.

Under the pseudonym Isak Dinesen, she published her first book, *Seven Gothic Tales*, when she was forty-eight years old. Her second book, *Out of Africa*, further established her reputation. Ernest Hemingway, accepting the Nobel Prize in 1954, said the prize should have gone instead to "that beautiful Danish writer Isak Dinesen."

Dinesen is quoted as saying, "I wrote a little every day without hope and without despair." She made her choice in the face of several obstacles. Her pledge, too, emerged over the course of a life against the odds.

Obstacles often require us to reroute our pledge. The obstacles may not be as catastrophic as the death of a lover and total financial ruin, but every path has them. Be not confused: having an obstacle to get around is not the same as failing. Failure calls for serious questioning; obstacles are simply part of your process. To continue, we learn to cope.

PRACTICE PUSHING BACK

Pushing against a fixed object is the physical equivalent of the emotional resolve we must have as we push against obstacles. Physical resistance is called *isometrics.* Like a pledge, the isometric grounding we gain by pushing into a wall or the floor can be thorough and unrelenting.

Remember, as a kid, pressing the back of your wrist against a wall for a minute or so, then stepping away and watching the stored power lift your arm of its own accord with no additional effort on your part? Static resistance training using the body's weight generates great power in the muscles. This is the basis of calisthenics.

Try simply pushing your palms together, fingers pointed upward. Press as hard as you can, as long as you can. By pulling your stomach in and curving your head forward, you can accomplish an upper-body stretch. The same stretch can be had by locking the fingers and pulling out with the arms.

Design your own isometric moves by pushing any part of your body against any surface. You can keep this resistance isolated, as pushing your hand into a wall for the muscles of the arm, or you can extend the resistance by pushing the feet into the ground and elongating all the muscles in the body.

Isometric stretches are fundamental and are done in nature by all living creatures, for pushing away from gravity is how we stand. Make a conscious effort to drive into the ground with your legs and feet. Then resist this movement by pulling your stomach back and your buttocks up. This will deliver a body-renewing stretch any time, any place.

Pushing forward in the face of resistance has powerful lifelong results. Take the Impressionist painter Claude Monet, for example. Monet made paintings in series, the same thing over and over again, whether it was cathedrals or haystacks or water lilies. As he aged, he began to suffer from macular degeneration. Bright light irritated his eyes, and it became painful to paint. His sense of depth was compromised, so in his later years, as he was painting water lilies, he began to paint them two-dimensionally and they began climbing the canvas vertically rather than lying horizontally in the pond. Also, he lost the ability to see whites, greens, and blues as clearly as he once had, so his paintings used more oranges, browns, and yellows. His strokes became less precise. Frustrated—so much so that he had two separate surgeries for cataracts—still he continued on.

Monet did not allow his difficulties to alter his pledge. In fact, the obstacles only increased the importance of his pledge as his body declined. Over a long career, he had developed habits and character that pushed him to resist the temptation to quit. His pledge yielded paradigm-shifting results as he helped lay the groundwork for the Cubist movement and art of the twentieth century.

Age is no excuse for inaction. I am over seventy-five now; I have good work habits, instilled early. No, I am not whacking out forty-eight *battements*, nor am I hurling my body in *jetés* through space (grrr). But I am still concerned about how movement shapes all of our lives and how I can help others understand this better. I adhere to my pledge to make a life in dance because I find lessons there that are fundamental in all of our lives and that I can learn nowhere else. With this book, I hope to share the recognition that you, too, are a body moving through time and space.

I made a choice that would evolve into a pledge over the course of my life. How do you get from choice to pledge? Push back against the obstacles, value your failures. Use everything you've got.

When the poet Donald Hall asked his friend, sculptor Henry Moore, for the secret to life, Moore—just turned eighty—had a quick pragmatic answer: "The secret of life is to have a task, something you devote your entire life to, something you bring everything to, every minute of the day for your whole life. And the most important thing is—it must be something you cannot possibly do!" Once a choice and never a goal—that's your pledge. Hand to heart, find your allegiance. Then keep reaching.

Chapter Three

Your Body Is Your Job

Exercise 3:   Marking Your Day   *Page 35*

I'm going to let you in on something: you actually already have a pledge. You live in your body. The care of your body has been entrusted to you, and only you—like it or not. How well are you keeping this pledge? It's your choice: do it well or do it badly.

You've heard it in one form or another a billion times. Your body is your job. If you don't work for it, it will not work for you.

The temptation to slacken physically increases with age. Kids just move—all the time. Then, later, we grow up and as stated, begin to hunch over our laptops, slouch on couches, and neglect our cores. Slowly our shoulders curl down, our spines concave, our necks turtle forward, persuading our bodies to constrict and occupy ever-shrinking airspace. Not pretty.

Ironically, the older we get, the more we should commit to physical activity—to slowing down the diminishment of our strength and agility, our bone density, our muscle mass, our elasticity, our recovery time. Getting physical and improving is how we can continue to thrive among the living.

For most people, being physical is something they do to work off restless energy or atone for self-indulgence. It's as if exercise is not supposed to interfere with more pressing responsibilities, such as making a living. Wrong! This is the universe turned upside down.

Dancers are lucky. Like all athletes, their profession requires them to drive their bodies to the limits of physical accomplishment every day of their careers. However, the rest of us are on our own time and our own dime to keep our bodies in good working order. Like a pledge, your devotion to your body requires daily renewal.

This is hard for many people to accept and even harder to put into practice. I blame this on a cultural bias that pits the challenges of mental acumen against the value of physical striving—and finds the physical to be of lesser value. It's a prejudice that says a gifted athlete cannot also be a superior intelligence. I've worked with elite athletes for decades—from NFL stars to Olympic figure skaters to amazing dancers—and I know this to be a false dichotomy. The greatest athletes are the sharpest minds, not the dullest. Their minds are tuned by physical activity—the way a regularly played piano stays in tune and a neglected instrument does not.

If you look at your body as a job, then gathering the discipline to stay strong and limber isn't a chore. Fitness expands our social, emotional, and intellectual well-being. It's how you pay and fulfill your obligations, craft your competitive edge, and elevate your self-esteem. When we make time for physical activity, whether it's a half-hour walk around the neighborhood, a sweaty workout with a trainer, or playing catch with our kids, we are not stealing from other parts of our lives. We are making it possible to live each day productively.

Let's not just burn calories. Let's use our calories. Many people think, "I should exercise because it will make me look better. That's why I'm burning calories." No, you're burning calories to acquire skills, and you're honing those skills with challenges you set up for yourself, for example, walking four more blocks a day or allowing yourself one more yoga session this week. Your exercising is always connected to a purpose and crafted to accomplish it. You must find purpose and put it to work.

As a dancer, I learned early to regard perpetual body work as spending and investing. I was working for the day at hand, yet also stockpiling my fitness and health for an uncertain future, developing the deepest possible reservoir of skill and conditioning that I could imagine to draw on as I aged—hopefully with compound interest. This has paid dividends. Integrating my body and my job focuses my day. It keeps me relatively energetic. It keeps me relatively in shape. It keeps me so that I can beat up most people. This is very useful. It is a powerful form of confidence.

Quirky billionaire Richard Branson credits his exercise regimen with increasing his productivity and giving him the energy he needs to maintain a demanding schedule. He begins each day with something physical. He is a tennis player, a biker, a runner, even a kitesurfer. His choice of activity is less important than his realization that it is crucial to his mind-set—so crucial that he wakes up at five a.m. in order to ensure that he has the time to include exercise in his day. He keeps his body fit and agile, thus supporting his mind.

When I look around my gym on Manhattan's Upper East Side, I see the routines of the other regulars revealing which elements of fitness matter to them. The burly barrel-chested financier going through his old-school regimen with heavy weights—squats, bench presses, curls—is focused on power. The female police officer cycling for thirty minutes, then attacking the weight machines, then finishing off with twenty minutes of stretching, is focused on flexibility, stamina, mobility, and power because she needs to project authority and readiness when she's on the job. The young attorney lifting dumbbells while balancing on a Bosu ball is developing coordination and balance for his golf game. The common thread among these people (I've been seeing them for years at the same morning hour) is a palpable sense of purpose.

They're not merely "getting in some exercise" when they can. They are as ambitious about taking control of their body as they are about succeeding at work. Their body is like a second career. Their reasons for being in the gym are as varied as their routines. Some are pursuing a physical ideal: a marathoner's whippet-thin profile, a dancer's elegant carriage, a power lifter's biceps. Some are rehabilitating ailing body parts or addressing health issues. Some seek to excel at a specific sport. All of them, however, are intimately and positively connected with their bodies. They know how to rotate their routines, focusing on different body parts each day, giving their muscles at least forty-eight hours of rest between heavy workouts. Like me, the regulars show up at the gym keeping a pledge to maximize, not squander, the healthy limbs they inherited at birth. They have eliminated inaction as an option.

William Pullen would agree that exercise elevates the mind. An avid runner, this British psychotherapist realized his mind reached a new plane of tranquility when he was out jogging. Finding that movement had much to teach him, he wondered, "Why learn only from the spoken word or thoughts when the body is so informative?" With a technique he termed *dynamic running therapy*, he was able to integrate running into his professional practice and his therapeutic method. He now uses DRT to help his patients deal with many forms of difficulty—from stress to depression to the ability to handle crisis. He has managed to integrate body and job beautifully.

Yes, I know. Trainers and gyms are expensive. Finding the time to bike or run is challenging. Working alongside others who are more adept and better-looking (everyone sees those around them as more attractive than themselves in one way or another) is intimidating. All in all, it is exhausting.

The fact is, we are all lazy—even me. I try not to beat myself up about it and neither should you. If you're not getting the exercise you need, you're far from alone: 1.3 billion people worldwide are not active enough to stave off preventable fatal diseases like heart disease and osteoporosis. According to the World Health Organization, the very minimum of physical activity you should aim for is one hundred fifty minutes of moderate exercise (like walking or swimming) or seventy-five minutes of vigorous exercise (such as running) a week. Before you object that you don't know how you would fit it in, consider: How much time do you spend watching Netflix? Or scrolling on your phone? This is a no-excuses situation. Your life is on the line.

It is hard work to keep a body taut and trim and in shape as you age. We all have an inherent resentment of the body's limits. After a couple of decades during which it functions flawlessly, we bump up against the point where it says, "No, thank you, this is as far as I go." A staircase we've climbed for years without thinking about it leaves us winded. We squint when reading the fine print. We develop a sudden affinity for scarves to cover the loose skin on our necks. Some deterioration is only natural, but other backsliding can be traced to our own behaviors, our own laziness.

As stated, I'm as lazy as the next person. But I am by now addicted to exercise. If I don't exercise, I feel slothful. There are days when I am flat. To be honest, one out of every three or four days I probably would like to say, *Okay, I don't feel like working today.* Then I go, *Fine. You don't work today, then you won't be able to work when you do feel like working. So, let's just go in and do our exercises, shall we?* I encourage you to do the same.

If you think you can't do it, at least try to imagine it. Jim Thorpe, a member of the Sac and Fox Nation, has been called the greatest athlete of the twentieth century, maybe of all time. He was a gold-medal Olympian, a champion at the decathlon, and a star NFL player, in addition to playing pro baseball and basketball. In 1912 he was on the deck of an ocean liner headed to the Stockholm Olympics. After noticing that Thorpe was sitting still while his fellow athletes exercised on the nearby track, a sports journalist asked him, "What are you doing, Jim? Thinking of your uncle Sitting Bull?"

"No," Thorpe said, "I'm practicing the broad jump. I've just jumped twenty-three feet, eight inches. I think that I can win it." He was putting himself through his paces mentally to prepare himself physically—and it paid off. He won the broad jump event in the decathlon a few weeks later and was lauded by the king of Sweden, "Sir, you are the greatest athlete in the world." Thorpe replied, "Thanks, King."

You and I probably will not take up the broad jump—or ocean-liner travel for that matter—but the practice of visualizing yourself doing something before you do it is a powerful way to get yourself moving even on days when you don't feel like it. Tomorrow, when you are waking up, before you even leave the bed, picture yourself going through an exercise routine—whatever it may be, a brisk walk, a run in the park, gardening, a game of pickup basketball—step by step. Be as specific as possible as you imagine exactly how you will move your body. You will be more likely to follow through with actually working out if you kick-start your brain into an active mind-set.

If setting aside a particular time of day to devote to exercise still feels like too much to you, there's a workaround for that, too. No excuses, no excuses, no excuses.

When I was just starting out as a dancer, I spent a lot of time on the subway with my fellow dancers. We were not idle on the platform, while waiting for our train to arrive. We were dancers, we moved. We'd be dancing, not full-out, but moving our bodies close to the vest, our movements restrained. The movement was small, and it didn't have the full blast of energy in it, but we did it in real time. It's a practice called *marking*, and we'd do it everywhere, all the time. We didn't want to waste a moment. Even sitting still, we'd be doing our steps, and the body was profiting as the train took us where we'd be working full-out that day.

——— MARKING YOUR DAY ———

Like the dancer, you have dozens of ways to mark your day—creative, substantial ways of integrating physical activity with whatever else occupies your time. Take the stairs instead of the elevator when you're shopping. Park in the farthest spot in the parking lot. Walk or bike to work. Practice keeping your abdominals engaged and your shoulders back during meetings.

Many of the most forward-thinking and employee-friendly companies offer fitness programs in the workplace—yoga, cardio classes, etc. The outdoor equipment company REI offers its employees two additional vacation days each year, but only if they are used to venture outdoors. Way to go.

Thinking of computer or desk work as one job and then exercise as another seems to me like holding two halves of a card deck in separate hands and then finding they need to be shuffled together. The more proficient the shuffle and the closer the cards cut together right hand to left, the better the deck is judged. So, too, we should think of cutting exercise in to our jobs as frequently as possible. Sitting, squirm more. Stand often to circle shoulders or pelvis. Find excuses to roam the hallways as often as possible. Go on a walk to take your phone calls. Sit less.

Waiting for the bus, bob, bend, and weave. This is also a good time to remind yourself that we breathe. Watch your rhythm: four counts in, four counts out. Allow yourself to increase this to six counts in and six counts out several times a day.

Learn to attach breathing to your work. Breathe in on the preparation for any physical effort and exhale on the actual activity. About to stand, take a deep breath. Exhale as you rise. All physical labor—from lifting ounces to hundreds of pounds—is best handled with this pattern to your breathing.

At work, break to stretch often—side, back, head, neck. Subvert stasis. Get a standing desk so that you can stand at your job whenever possible—all this will help eliminate the division created when we separate exercise from our jobs. Making your job into exercise will not replace the gym, but it will help keep you alive.

When you approach the care and feeding of your body as a job—a second career equivalent in value to all the other ways you pay the bills—you are channeling a farmer's work ethic. I liken fitness to farming. A farmer does the same two things every day: show up to work and adapt to what he finds there. A farmer's life—raising animals, milking cows, cultivating crops—is the quintessential physical life. The hours are grueling, there are no off days, there's always more to do, it's dangerous (more lethal than any other occupation), and the entire enterprise can be wiped out in a flash at the whimsy of Mother Nature. Yet the farmer persists in this onerous activity, usually well into old age, because there is sensory delight in growing things and renewal in each season's arrival (not to mention honor in feeding people). The rewards outweigh the grinding rigors and unwelcome surprises, and in fact are more precious because of the hardships met and overcome.

So, pick your poison. Run, lift weights, dance, swim, skate, broad-jump. Make a commitment and practice it regularly, same time, same place. Your track, gym, studio, pool, all can become your sanctuary. In a volatile universe, a ten-pound iron weight is a constant. It puts you in the now. It's unyielding and pitiless but also generous, even comforting. And it is nonjudgmental. You either lift the weight or you don't. If you do it well, your reward is more weight. The weight doesn't transform. You do.

Here's what I know: a life that gives the body its due is a happy life. Yes, your hours are grim. Your markers for success usually involve exhaustion. The promise of decline leers around every corner. The threat of injury hovers over you. I used to believe it was a satisfying life despite these drawbacks. Now I see it's because of them. You've got to make your obstacles into your collaborators. No excuses.

Chapter Four

Make Change Your Habit

K eep reaching.

This is the goal of any pledge. It connects us to forward movement, which puts time on our side. Put it there, keep it there.

The first thing any sailor must do before setting sail is hoist anchor. In our metaphor, you are the sailor, and the anchor is the weight of your past. While we have no past when we are born, it accumulates every day thereafter. Piling it up can bring, with luck, wealth and adventures. But living in your past can also make you stodgy and immobile.

Take Lot's wife from Genesis 19. Planning to destroy the corrupt city of Sodom, God sends two angels to warn Lot, the one good man living there, to leave with his family immediately. They are specifically instructed not to look back as they flee, but Lot's wife cannot help herself. Glancing over her shoulder, she sees everything she has ever known go up in flames. For returning to her past, she is turned into a pillar of salt—probably, I have always imagined, from evaporating tears.

Lot's wife pivots on the tragic. But what of those folks who reside happily, even smugly, in the comfort zone of the familiar?

We all know people who prefer life in the yesteryear. Their now is then.

Take what I call the Dylan cult. In my generation, many people have stalled in the 1960s. Over half a century later, their thinking, values, and styles are still permeated by the spirit of the Summer of Love. These folks require every rendition of "The Times They Are a-Changin' " to be the exact iconic bootleg they first heard in 1964. Anything else is a betrayal of their youth. As with the baseball enthusiast remembering stats, there is something charmingly sentimental in this exercise, but to stay in the past is to be doomed. Baseball has moved on, Dylan has moved on, only they have not?

The peril of nostalgia is the way it arrests evolution. Have you ever found yourself using the phrase "I'm one of those people who [fill in the blank]": "needs to have a plan for everything," "hates change," "loves to go against the current," "is always anxious"? Doubtless you have come to think of yourself thus because of experiences you've had, and you're likely right that, at one time or another, you may have indeed been a person who . . . However, it's worth taking a look at whether those qualities still apply to you today or whether you are relying on a shopworn idea of yourself.

Unless we embrace the condition of change, the past will act as an anchor, preventing growth. I've always been an advocate of habit—but with time, unchecked or unnoticed habits will hold you back.

What if you were to make change your actual habit instead?

Not an easy chore. We know ourselves by what we have been and done—what we have accomplished and the experiences we have had. Yet we can also be stopped cold by feeling we have much to lose if we let the past be left behind.

How can we become comfortable with change in order to remain one step ahead of what is past? Here are five suggestions.

1. Take On a Persona

Identity can be an attachment that holds you back, just as surely as an overdose of nostalgia. Maybe you think of yourself as an extrovert or a day-dreamer or type A. Yes, having a clear sense of yourself is closely related to having confidence and good self-esteem. But when was the last time you decided to opt out of something because it "wasn't like you"? Stay in the past, choose not to change, and like Lot's wife, you will remain immobile, frozen in place, looking to stop time and going not much of anywhere. Hand in glove with your archnemesis, status quo bias.

Learn to imagine yourself differently. Look to the example of Hokusai, the Japanese woodcutter of the eighteenth century, who had a process that allowed him to sail through life without getting caught in his past. He shifted his identity and his style constantly, using more than thirty names in his lifetime. He moved frequently, immersing himself in a whole new atmosphere, finding novel subject matter—whether it was courtesans, peasants, or, most famously, Mount Fuji—reordering his entire lifestyle. For him, renaming and shifting identity was a lifelong practice. This process allowed him to be productive over a very long while, impacting even today—his invention of manga is still alive in contemporary cartoons—on how we see things.

Another polymorph, Robert Zimmerman, came to New York City in 1963. Ten years later, he left as Bob Dylan. By splitting himself into person and persona, he was able to compartmentalize. Robert Zimmerman, the person, had responsibilities, obligations, and a somewhat predictable existence. Bob Dylan, the persona, did not. Zimmerman could give Dylan permission to try anything, sending him out to test the waters of opportunity the way miners test the oxygen in a mine by sending in a canary first. (Most handy when the criticism is bad. Then Zimmerman can say, "Wasn't me, Dylan did it.")

While most of us don't go to the extreme of creating a persona, it can be useful to think of a before and after. The moment you marry, have a child, divorce. Even if you do not actually take on a new name, give yourself the option, with a milestone, to adopt a generational tag. Before a certain event, you are Jane the First. After this event, you are Jane the Second. Passing beyond an event of major significance—such as childbirth or a major surgery—gives you the right to behave differently.

At the other end of the spectrum, you might try dissolving your identity completely. I've always been fascinated by Sergio Leone's "Man with No Name" trilogy of movies from the 1960s, starring Clint Eastwood. The first film, *A Fistful of Dollars*, sets the pattern for its sequels (*For a Few Dollars More* and *The Good, the Bad, and the Ugly*). Eastwood plays a mysterious unnamed gunslinger who inserts himself into a gang war, playing each side off the other. He settles some debts on both sides and then rides out of town. It's mythmaking storytelling, based on Akira Kurosawa's classic, *Yojimbo*. We know nothing about the hero at the start and just as little at the end. He rarely speaks, gives nothing away about where he came from, what he has done, or who he is. He is named Nobody, defined not by his past but only by his actions in the present.

What would happen if you went into your next meeting, sales call, or social situation determined to emulate Eastwood: no past, no list of credits, no reputation, not even a name. You cannot reveal or use anything from your past—not what you do, where you went to college, who you know. Your only revelations involve the present or future. Would that work for you or against you? Would the situation be good, bad, or ugly? Your objective is to free yourself to be whatever and whoever you need to be right now.

DROP THE PAST BY LETTING GO

Here is a simple exercise that allows you to stand in the middle of your living room and challenge your status quo by changing your physical center.

Stay firmly planted with your weight evenly distributed between both feet.

As ever, be aware of your breathing: in on the work, out on the release.

Take your arms into a high V with an inhale. Then exhale and let the arms flop.

Next, reach your arms out from each shoulder to both sides on the inhale, then exhale, letting the arms cross the front of your body as you drop. Bend your knees with the drop.

Last, lift both arms to the left side and inhale; exhale, dropping your arms across to the right, bending your knees. Then reverse to the right.

Repeat this set of three until your body has memorized what to do next without the brain having to think. Your body makes its own connections.

Now we'll widen your center by swinging. First, broaden your stance. Then drop your whole torso, bending over your knees in one flop. That's your new center. Swing your torso to the right and then the left. Having your weight down the middle or off to the side of your center changes what we call your *placement*, where you carry your weight in your feet and legs.

These are different identities for your body. Be aware that being very grounded conveys a sense of confidence and security that is slightly diminished when you are off center. Think of locating a new center as finding a new you for the day. Shall you be striding forth strongly or—pitched slightly forward or back—just a tad vulnerable? Each placement has its advantages for both your skeleton and your character. You will feel it, others will see it.

Carried to an extreme, being too far off your center is but a way station to a fall. This you can use as a heads-up to go with the flow. While I am not looking to promote falling in your life, if you feel a fall coming, here's a clue. Try not to fight back.

2. Have the Courage to Fail

We fear letting go; we worry that in leaving our past for the unknown, we will fail along the way. What if we do? There is no growth without risk. Remember as children, learning to walk, we faced risk bravely. Watch closely: you'll see kids fall often and, most of the time, without injury.

Can this capacity be maintained as we get older? Bones grow brittle, our muscles lose the mass to cushion the fall and our bodies the flexibility to descend with grace. Done accidentally, falling is a dangerous thing and rightfully avoided whenever possible. But done with control, it is empowering. If you expect to fall, are prepared to fall, or can accept a fall and do not resent what appears to be a loss of control, you will find the body much more capable of coping with losing its balance. Being able to fall physically is a sign of strength. Both failing and falling are specialized genres of action, and handled well, both are an art form. The Japanese hold special classes in the techniques of falling for their elders, a demographic held in high esteem by their culture.

The key to all well-executed physical falls is in their recovery. If you know how you are getting up from your fall, you will feel better on the way down. There are many varieties of fall, but all have one basic requirement: you cannot hesitate on the way down. You must relax into the fall and let it go straight to its mark. Resisting on the way down causes injury.

Knowing how we are getting up makes falling so much more welcoming. Check out Buster Keaton's pratfalls on YouTube. The five-minute reel of Keaton's best stunts will make you wince with their brutality and then smile shortly thereafter. The tragedy of the fall is turned around swiftly each time by Keaton's rebound. Once knocked to the ground, Keaton never stayed down long. He always used the momentum of his fall to recover, usually in the very next frame. But of course, in his case, he planned the disasters of the past—his falls to the ground—for their spectacular escapes into a future. He always knew where he was going before he fell. Like Keaton, you can take the mystery out of letting go by thinking ahead. Imagining yourself in a future makes leaving the past more appealing. Be brave. Hit the deck without pause. Use your momentum down for your recovery. That's the only way it works.

The same is true of your decision-making process. Hesitation can cause injury.

3. Combating Procrastination to Create Change

A major obstacle to action—and thus change—is procrastination. Some people are lazy (they put off work). Some are overly ambitious (they commit to more work than they can handle). Some lack the confidence to act. Some fear failure, manufacturing conditions that make success impossible. Some need more data and more planning before they're ready to work (and there's never enough data). Some have too many distractions luring them away from what they should be doing. It's all the same.

We tend to think of procrastination exclusively as a short-run issue and fail to detect the damage it does to our long-term prospects. For example, we all want financial security and know that saving money for our later years is the best way to achieve it. But short-term needs appear—a vacation, a better car, a family emergency—so we delay putting money away. It's always something. This is how long-term goals are overwhelmed by short-term considerations. If we can't get past the distraction of immediate gratification in the short run, we have no chance of creating a solid long run.

The procrastinators among us prefer to put off until later rather than acting now. Studies show that the procrastinator's brain is very good at feeling future rewards without doing the work. Jane the Procrastinator can become Jane the Second without passing the trial because she already feels the reward to come without experiencing the ordeal. I'm afraid this is not how things happen. A good scare might prompt action for Jane, but short of that, here's a thought.

Facing any onerous or unappealing task (the kind you always put off), ask yourself: How little can I tolerate right now? In other words, what's the least I can do to get started? We procrastinate because our tolerance for what lies ahead is compromised. The task is too daunting or time-consuming or frustrating. We don't file our tax return on time because gathering the scattered stubs and receipts is annoying. We don't write the term paper because the prospect of sitting alone in front of our laptop is intimidating.

What I'm recommending is thinking small—very small—so you can ignore the real or imagined monumentality of what you're facing. If you're supposed to be writing a lengthy report, what's the bare minimum you can do on day one? Assemble your research? Create a file system for your notes? On day two, do the bare minimum again. Write a paragraph? Write an outline? And so on, until you're deep enough into the project that forward momentum is unavoidable. For the procrastinator, the only bad choice is no choice.

4. Beware Entitlement

Accumulated successes, whether baby steps or big leaps forward, can create a creeping entitlement where we start to believe the world owes us. Earning success becomes expecting it.

Few of us are spared. Creeping entitlement is why we get angry at friends who don't respond to our calls or emails immediately (our time is precious; we should not be kept waiting). Or why we justify any of our selfish or hurtful actions by telling ourselves, "I'm worth it."

Entitlement is way more disabling than empowering. At first, it makes us sloppy. We cut corners, bend the rules to suit ourselves, and assume we can get away with it. Sloppiness becomes our "new normal." Eventually, entitlement stops us in our tracks.

Get out of your own way; do not expect what you have been in the past to make your today. The wealth of our past does not entitle us to anything other than—with luck—another shot at tomorrow. Do not believe that if you set the target in the past, envisioned the result, prepared for it, executed on point, and made it happen that the universe is now whispering in your ears, *You were right. How'd you get to be so clever?*

Creeping entitlement is not an issue when I'm confined to the relatively meager resources of the dance world. Frankly, there's not enough money in dance to permit the queenly extravagances of limousines or wasted rehearsal periods that I regard as entitlement. Every hour and penny must be accounted for. Things change in the bigger-budget environments of Hollywood and Broadway, where creature comforts are abundant and whims are blithely indulged. It's very easy to go from being grateful that an assistant asks if you'd like some coffee to demanding a freshly ground cup as your birthright. You don't even notice that you're changing. That's how creepy entitlement can be.

I wage my war on entitlement on two fronts. It begins with physical self-reliance. I open my own doors, carry my own bags, place my own phone calls, answer all emails, and eat my own cooking. I don't cancel appointments without an extraordinary reason (and I expect the same courtesy in return). I don't exempt myself from the rules that I expect everyone else to follow (I'm special, but not that special!). These are personal strategies that consistently snap me back to now, reminding me that from moment to moment, all I'm entitled to is the desire to do my best.

5. Change by Knowing When It's Over

Learning to recognize the end is a skill that comes with age. When you are still young, being able to recognize that the past is complete is a rare accomplishment. Few see the endpoint when there is still so much of the future ahead.

However, record-breaking runner-turned-physician Roger Bannister did just this in 1954. As millions of people around the world followed his seemingly impossible quest to break the four-minute mile—without any sponsorships or coaching network to sustain him—Bannister coordinated his already brutal training regimen with a life outside the sport. He integrated his workouts with the rigorous demands of medical school, squeezing in his runs during his lunch break at a track two train stops away from St. Mary's Hospital, where he was a student.

Pursuing his mostly self-designed and imposed regimen, Bannister broke the four-minute mile with a time of 3:59:4. Spectacular. He was recognized around the world for the achievement. But practically the next day, following just two more races, he reported back to work at St. Mary's. Showing a thorough grasp of the need to move forward with his life, as well as a good deal of perspective and humility, he said, "Now life in earnest was beginning."

Making an adjustment of this magnitude from one area of accomplishment to another requires both courage and confidence. For Bannister, this was a huge adaptation. Here you had a guy who was acknowledged as the fastest man on the face of the earth, treated like an international hero, and suddenly he is going back to medical school to become a professional like everybody else. How does that work? You might guess that the answer is anticipation. Bannister had already laid the groundwork for his next step when he enrolled in medical school years earlier. He kept going, making his second act not just longer but more satisfying than his first. He was later quoted as saying, "I'd rather be remembered for my work in neurology than my running. If you offered me the chance to make a great breakthrough in the study of the automatic nerve system, I'd take that over the four-minute mile right away. I worked in medicine for sixty years. I ran for about eight."

But note: the corner that Bannister turned was not a total disconnect. They rarely are. Both running and doctoring expressed his intention and his pledge to investigate the workings of the human body. It was all the same practice to him. If his path were to be mapped, imagine the yin/yang symbol and then trace it with your finger. You will find that if you start clockwise on the circle, you will finish counterclockwise. Sometimes a path that makes sense in hindsight could never be comprehended at its start. When making big choices in our lives, the best course is to recognize continuity in our intention. Thus we are neither repudiating nor repeating the past but, rather, respecting it as we move on. Each day prepares your next.

W hether it's worshipping Dylan, reliving your high school football years, or trying to fit in to your old jeans, nostalgia encourages us to recall days when surely we were better off—younger, more potent, happier, even perhaps taller. Visiting the past has its place in a life well lived, but a visit to the past needs to be exactly that—a visit. Your past is past. Let's learn to leave it there. This, too, is a discipline.

The two people I know who best exemplify a comfortable existence visiting the past, yet living in the present, are Marilyn and Irving Lavin. We've been friends so long that none of us remembers how we met. Both are noted classicists and distinguished art historians—he a revered Bernini expert and emeritus scholar at Princeton's Institute for Advanced Study, she an expert on Piero della Francesca. Irving is eighty-nine, Marilyn ninety-one.

Irving and Marilyn are trained to deal with the past. They go in, look at what's there, analyze it, and pull what they can use into now. For scholars, this is a daily practice. While the Lavins are fluent in the historical past, their comfort zone is the present: they hike, ski, and fully exist in the now, without fear. I witnessed how this fearlessness keeps stagnation away one Sunday in early spring 2016. They drove from Princeton to a village in the Catskills, where I was entrenched for six weeks to work. After watching rehearsals, we took long walks through the area's fields and hills. I noticed their vigorous disregard for where they planted their feet in the muddy ground, heedless of the possibility of a sprained ankle or knee. Coping with the consequences of the future unknown is part of their adventure. This is growth, and they take a small step in that direction daily.

The Lavins, grounded in a marriage of sixty-six years, still find novelty in one another's company as they awake every morning at the same time and poke each other, asking, "Are you still alive?" And then Marilyn tells Irving, "Get up, Irving, start the day." A little poke is a great beginning for large discoveries.

Chapter Five

Kick into High Gear

Exercise 5: Jump For Joy *Page 60*

A small poke in the ribs from a loved one may help set the tone for the day once your eyes are open. But if we are to aim higher than "I'm alive," a jolt with more serious voltage may then be required.

Whatever is going on when I wake up in the morning, I engage in an all-over body assessment. Like a pilot checking the dials in the cockpit before takeoff, I check in with my muscles, my ligaments, my mood. Some mornings, I'm feeling spirited and ready to address the day, but others, I would prefer to tug the blankets up over my head and hide from every one of my thoughts and obligations. When I am feeling flat and blah, I realize this is going to be one of those days when I will have to pull out a stop and kick it up a gear.

Optimism is a choice, and it's yours to make. You want a victory-lap kind of outcome to your day, you gotta work for it. Extreme measures may be called for.

Going for a dive into the deep end of the day right off the bat, one cup of coffee down and another close at hand, I get to my stereo and, as quickly as possible, cut to the chase. On the days when you need all the help you can get, nothing promotes the victory rush like certain pieces of music. Think fast tempi, lots of volume and upward chromatic progressions. I put on circus marches, my all-time favorite go-to piece of music when I feel shitty and that is just too bad. John Philip Sousa, college fight songs, national anthems. Fight. Fight. Fight. And always in a major key. No room for minor-key downers here. Failure is not an option.

Music blasting, I direct myself to my home studio and get moving. I might start out sluggish—even begin at the other end of my energy spectrum with a slow stretch or two, feeling a bit like a woolly mammoth unfreezing from its block of ice—but after a few bars of letting the bold rhythms course through my veins, I am feeling more ready to face the day. As hokey as it sounds, there simply cannot be sustained forward movement in your life without the energy that optimism brings. Who wants to work toward failure?

JUMP FOR JOY

Jumping is one of the greatest movements the body has for building and expressing optimism. We all know this—jacks jump, ropes jump, frogs, horses, kangaroos, everybody jumps—so let's take off now. But it requires energy, and you are going to have to practice building it like anything else.

Here are three different jumps to get you started. If you are a novice, try them in three stages: practice them first with your fingers, and then use feet still seated. Next get up. No music yet.

- Jump One: Sky Jump

  Stand with both feet together. Bend your knees. Jump straight up. Reach to the heavens with your arms. Repeat many times—at least three.

- Jump Two: Ski Jump

  Feet together, jump out to the right; arms go high to your left. Then jump back to center. Reverse. Repeat. Many times—at least four.

- Jump Three: March in Place

    Feet slightly apart, weight on your right, lift your left knee high. Then jump onto your left foot and bring your right knee high and slap that knee with the opposite hand. And reverse. Repeat many times. Try six.

- Jump Four: Traveling

    First to the front, weight on your right foot, jump forward to the left foot. From there back to the right foot. Then place both feet together. Reverse. Go for four each leg.

    Same pattern, only now jump to the side, right and left. And then to the back. Repeat many times. Try eight. Note, as ever: the body prefers moving forward to going backward.

Now let's really kick it up a gear and mix in the music.

Here are three samples of irresistible can-do music.

Go for stomps and joys—stomps and joys are literal dance forms, like the minuet or gigue—high-energy New Orleans marches full of energy. Try "Boogaboo," a joy by Jelly Roll Morton, and jump. Or "Stompin' at the Savoy" by Louis Armstrong. Do what it says.

Try on a jump blues such as Lionel Hampton's "Flying Home." I defy you to stand still. Jumps are jitterbug, and it is that high velocity and power that got us through World War II.

Then there is always the Ur powerhouse march, the finale of Beethoven's Ninth Symphony, "Ode to Joy." The chorus in the last movement, combined with Beethoven's messianic power, confirms the human potential within us all. This piece is guaranteed to stir you to a recognition of the power that music has to inspire us and get us going.

> You can, of course, choose whatever music you like. Look for the maximum-octane music your body already has loaded in its muscle memory from past listenings, then get jumping. It's visceral; the body takes over and the brain takes a rest. Your reward will be the runner's endorphins. Literally get high: jump.

What do I mean by "kick into high gear"? So far I have boxed "Take Up Space," "Mark Your Day," "Let It Go." Now, with "Jump For Joy," you get the picture: the boxes are your verb area. Action in considered motion means dance, so yes, I am indeed reminding you that you, too, my dearest reader are a dancer. And while you're at it, why not maximize the power input and do it with a community of others?

I have a civilian friend—as we refer to nondancers in my world— who, at age seventy, just signed up for square dancing. Another pal went for Israeli folk dance. Modern dance? Ballet for beginners? Why not? It may not be a pretty picture, but so what? Give it a try. Flushed from pumping, you will be heated, sweating and miles away from any bleakness you might have come in with. If you don't think dancing is your thing, go for doubles tennis or pickup basketball. Find a group activity with momentum, the key factor to keeping old age away. Don't just hit a couple of positions—stir things up. Unleash some joy with a community of like-minded souls.

I look for optimism when I select my dancers. All successful dancers I know realize they will not "win" the battle against age, but this does not stop them from working hell for leather now, full commitment.

Using optimism as fuel, they choose to dance, fully aware that the time will come when they cannot continue professionally. But up until that time, they are the immortals who, like gods and young children, can be asked to do anything and will find a way. They will put on a show for the folks, and the folks will come along, and in this, there is joy and purpose. You will never find a negative dancer who is working well. Doesn't exist. Can't exist. What they do is way too difficult to also sustain a negative mind-set. In working with groups, I have always found that a committed dancer with a positive attitude is more to our advantage than a difficult one with massive talents.

As you move, allow only positive images—adoring crowds yelling, hard-won fights where failure is not an option—to help you turn up the heat and drive harder. High gear is not only faster, it has more power. It is where we have to be in order to accomplish really tough jobs. Believe in yourself and your purpose and keep it going. And talk to the body with kind words—at least as encouraging as you would use to support your best friend. Learn to become your own cheerleader.

We all had ideas of what our life would look like when we were younger, and sometimes it is a tremendous drain on our motivation to look at where we've landed and find ourselves short of our intended destination. Maybe you thought you'd be the head of your department by now. Or that you'd have found time to play an instrument. Or that you'd have a partner who loves to travel as much as you do. Yes, it sucks when life doesn't turn out how we'd have liked, but tough luck.

Too often, aging can promote a condition identified by psychologists at the University of Pennsylvania as *learned helplessness*. This shows up when we are conditioned to expect pain or discomfort and we make a peremptory retreat to avoid those nasty outcomes. We see no way to escape, thus become defeated, acting as though we are completely helpless. In one experiment, young elephants were tied to posts with thick ropes to train them not to escape. Later in life, these elephants, much stronger, required only a small line to hold them fast. They will not even try to break free. Believing we cannot change our outcome leads to lethargy. Negativity and stagnation go hand in hand. We learn to stay put.

The way to boost your mood for real, in a sustained way, is to line up your actions and your values. Practice optimism. Torpor creeps in when we approach our daily lives with dread, and dread emerges when we do not support our pledge. Could we have forgotten our pledge? Go back and look at it now. Where are you coming up short? What in your life is not contributing to fulfilling it? What can you plug into to regain your focus? Short on energy? Go for the marches.

Is optimism more difficult with age? A bit. Philip Roth liked to stare down his face in the mirror early in the morning when he was working and say, "Attack, attack." Richard Avedon insisted, "Each shoot must be thrilling." Over long careers, this pair never quit demanding more from their life and work. As time went by, they found refuge and perhaps, even on occasion, a bit of revenge by cranking up the optimism. Their discipline was fierce. The tougher it gets, the more positive you need to be.

Still, even for the faithful, there will be whining days. There will be kvetching. That's your cue to get funny. Go to laughter; the implosion releases huge energy.

Michael Wex, in *Born to Kvetch*, tells an anecdote about a man on a train complaining loudly and repeatedly, "Oy, I am thirsty." Over and over, the man complains about his thirst, until a fellow passenger can take it no longer and fetches the man a cup of water. The man drinks it, then promptly says, "Oy, was I thirsty." Amusing yes, but illustrative also. It demonstrates two truths about our kvetching: sometimes we get so attached to our grievances that we hate to give them up, and the best person to address the complaint is the complainer.

I fancy myself a stoic, able to endure pain and difficulty. It comes with the territory in dance: we expect to be exhausted. But as I was writing this book, a friend pointed out how much complaining I was doing about my crowded schedule and feeling overloaded.

I had a meltdown day. So I invited my friend, someone from the old school who I knew had been having a hard time herself, to join me for dinner. I figured we'd be misery buddies. When I got to the restaurant, they didn't want to seat me without her, so I was already in a snit by the time she arrived. Once she sat down and asked how it was going, I laid in. "How's it going?" I said. "It's going for shit." *Kvetch, kvetch, kvetch.*

She looked across the table at me and said, "You've become timid. I don't like to see you being meek." That was all it took—a sudden flip to see what I looked like from the other side of the table. Had I succumbed to a bout of learned helplessness? Where was my pledge? Jeez Louise. She was right. I'd been on a negativity bender.

When I catch myself kvetching, I try to zoom out, to place myself in the audience of my life so I can get a little perspective—is this a woe worth addressing?—and to determine if I can fix it. That's where a good kvetch can be useful—it can hit a truth on the head using humor as a hammer. When I find myself kvetching, I ask, *Is this something I can change?* If not, then I try to shut up and move on and in so doing, set to work on improving my lot.

In 1981, when I was working with legendary actor, song-and-dance man Donald O'Connor, in London during the shoot for the film of *Ragtime*, he was featured in a number with twenty young ladies. It was always O'Connor at the age of fifty-six (and following health issues, in a corset to help support his weight), who was on his feet first. Unlike the girls, he never marked a moment in a single rehearsal. He was full-out every time—wholehearted every time. He simply did not let down. Fortitude in spades. Growing up in vaudeville, he had a real trooper's attitude: nothing would stop him. He was from the Buster Keaton school of hard knocks and his attitude was that you don't get out of a show unless you die. The man was bursting with optimism. Like they say, dying is easy, comedy is hard.

O'Connor understood that to produce positive feelings, you gotta work. He was the guy who, after filming one of Hollywood's most demanding solos in half a day—"Make 'Em Laugh," for *Singin' in the Rain*—spent the next three days in bed recovering. When he returned to work, he was told that the film had fogged and he would have to reshoot. Right. The show goes on. A given. He didn't kvetch. He went back to work.

When you are kvetching, ask yourself, *What are you complaining about?* What is the change that you would like to see happen? Is it something you can fix? Then fix it. Beware making plans that require coordinated efforts with other people, a protracted time line, elaborate equipment, multiple authorities or experts. I repeat: find what you can do for yourself and then fix it.

It was you, my friend, I remind myself, *who made this choice.* So when you find yourself grousing, my tough-love advice: pull up your socks.

Ironically, protecting our hard-won positivity gains is sometimes best done by learning how to say no. As important as it is to boost your energy with positivity, it is equally important to cut the negative energy from your life. Whether it is an overcrowded schedule, a terrible diet, or giving in to boredom, you need to learn how to say no.

The older I get, the more I say no. I turn down jobs, invitations, interviews, you name it. We usually have a list of good reasons when we accept a new challenge. But we only need one reason—some factor that makes success impossible—to decline. I didn't appreciate this way back when. I'd dive in to a new situation, ignoring the killer flaw that doomed the enterprise, believing I could overcome it, or that things would change for the better, or I'd get lucky. I was seduced by the glamour of difficulty—and what's more glamorous than "impossible" or never done before? It was like climbing Mount Everest and praying for a life-threatening storm to make the ascent more meaningful or dramatic. It rarely turned out well. Afterward I'd reproach myself, *Why didn't I trust the voice that said I'm wasting time?* Do this enough times and you learn to walk away instead of diving in.

It applies, too, in personal relationships. A friend becomes too demanding, or unreliable, or self-pitying. When you're inexperienced, you think you can change that person, so you hang in there far beyond what's healthy for you. Or, if you end the friendship, you worry you have failed. Not so.

We all have friends or relatives who raise the negativity level in the room because they're pessimistic, contrary, belligerent, opinionated, incurious, uninformed, or otherwise unpleasant. We're obliged to see them at holidays and social gatherings and make a mental note to steer clear. I have a label for such people: dopamine-negative. The adrenaline surge around them is competitive and unwelcome. It becomes a quest for survival. We don't get the feel-good chemical blast in their company that being willing to connect with others delivers.

On the other hand, we all know people who put a smile on our faces. We look forward to seeing them with the same fizzy excitation that children feel on Christmas Eve. Their presence is a gift. These are dopamine-positive people. However we define good chemistry, we have it with them.

We need to practice this state of being with like-minded souls in all aspects of our lives, from our careers to our friends. They needn't be cheerful buffoons, but neither should they be so burdened by complaint and negative energy that they drain yours. Harsh as it may sound, this is not a completely outrageous way to segregate your universe of relationships. We already do this intuitively when we gravitate to cliques of like-minded people at work or rope off a few weekends each year just to spend time with our best friend from college.

What if we formalized the process? Is there a benefit to identifying who it is we are eager to see?

Divide a page into two columns. On the right side, list all the people whose appearance you anticipate with pleasure. On the left side, list those you anticipate with dread. The only criterion here is the dopamine rule. Anticipating each person either gives you a positivity blast or doesn't. You're not judging people's social grace or sweet temper or agreeability, only your level of engagement around them. My dopamine-positive side includes a few curmudgeons. Crankiness doesn't mean they're not stimulating.

Next, calculate how much time you spend with people in each group. This is the telling part, the only reason for this exercise. Are you surrounding yourself with people who bring the best out of you or wasting time with people who bring you down? Now that you know, how do you feel about it?

Give yourself permission to say no next time to one of the people on the left side of your paper when they ask you to spend time with them.

After a career of immense productivity as a sculptor and painter of prodigious gifts, Henri Matisse found himself essentially bedridden at the age of seventy-two. First diagnosed with abdominal cancer in

1941, he lived until 1954, creating many works in his last years. Recalling the assemblages he made during his Fauve period half a century earlier, Matisse found new possibilities for working by using his scissors. Lying on his back in bed, with a twelve-foot bamboo cane strapped to his wrist, he was able to paste huge swaths of colored paper on his walls to create works of extraordinary sophistication and joy. His purpose remained strong and when he died he left, taped to his wall, a maquette for a stained-glass window that would be executed two years later.

Fight fight fight—keep chipping at the status quo bias, keep chipping at the funk. Fight fight fight until you can make change—not stasis—the constant. Ultimately your values, faith, beliefs most dearly held are what will support your finale. Visualize. Remember your pledge.

In 1908, when he was just beginning to work as an artist, Matisse wrote, "My destination is always the same but I work out different routes to get there." In a life filled with many difficulties—cancer, world war, painful divorce—Matisse's work never abandoned his pledge to find joy in the world around him. "What I dream of is an art of balance, purity and serenity. Devoid of troubling or depressing subject matter." In late photographs by Henri Cartier-Bresson, Matisse holds a living dove in his left hand and, with his right, sketches this bird as an exuberant celebration of life. Ultimately, optimism is a discipline and it was this that steeled Matisse to work through his very last days. "There are always flowers for those who want to see them."

Chapter Six

Hope Less, Plan More

Exercise 6: Daily Pact to Share *Page 84*

Along with millions and millions of other readers, I am a huge fan of Agatha Christie novels. There are sixty-six of them, and each—nearly all in the genre known as "closed room" murder mysteries—delivers a universe rich in possibilities: anyone could have done it, no one did it, everyone did it. Red herrings and twists of all shapes and sizes emerge, but ultimately, the crime will have its one and only inevitable resolution. Throughout, our anticipation will be teased knowingly but never dishonestly. Cramming the early chapters with information and drama, the later ones dole it out more conservatively, and readers, hooked on the pleasure of making discoveries, enjoy the slowed pace. Christie's skillful use of anticipation makes the novels addictive. She knows how to make you want to keep going.

The older you get, the more you need motivation to keep going. Anticipation is a powerful prod. Like all motivators, anticipation works on the pleasure principle—the desire to increase pleasure, decrease pain. Often what we anticipate is a desirable occasion: a reunion, a vacation, a second date, the prospect of sex. As Samuel Johnson said, "Few enterprises of great labor or hazard would be undertaken if we had not the power of magnifying the advantages we expect from them."

Some years ago I mentioned to a biologist friend how listless and uninspired I felt on days when I had nothing scheduled. I'd figured the opposite should be true, that I'd enjoy the break from a typical day's demands. "Isn't a holiday for rest, relaxation, and feeling better?" I asked.

He explained my dilemma via neurochemistry. Our brains are wired to seek a reward. When we work toward a goal and achieve it—a big goal like landing a promotion or small one like being on time to our kid's recital—a part of our brain (specifically, our frontal cortex) is bathed with dopamine, which stimulates our pleasure centers. We catch on quickly to this reward system: do the work, get rewarded with a feel-good blast of dopamine.

But it's a more complex scenario than "do this, get that," as Swiss scientists demonstrated when they studied lab monkeys by hooking them up to electrodes that monitor dopamine activity. A light cues a monkey to press a lever and after a few seconds delay, a bit of food drops down as reward. You'd expect the greatest dopamine activity at the moment of reward. But in fact, the dopamine release peaks right after the light signal and before the monkey presses the lever. The pleasure produced by dopamine isn't about reward. It's about the anticipation of reward.

Our motivation, said my friend, is governed by anticipation. It sags when we have nothing to look forward to. It fades after we're rewarded for doing the work. It peaks somewhere in the middle when we are flush with feelings of expectation and confidence that a reward is coming.

Consider the story "Babette's Feast" by our friend Isak Dinesen. Babette is a maid who works for two elderly sisters. After she wins a sum of money in a lottery, they assume she will take her leave of them, but instead, she uses her windfall to prepare an elaborate multi-course meal of turtle soup, blinis with caviar, and quail with truffle sauce for her employers. Her sole reward is anticipating the pleasure of her audience.

Dangerous as it may be to interpret behavior solely through neuro-chemical reactions, I could now understand my lethargy on empty days. I was suffering from dopamine deprivation because I had nothing to antic-ipate. I missed the blast.

Any time we reach from a beginning to a goal far forward—say, solv-ing a crime or continuing to uphold a pledge for many years—it is antic-ipation that will keep us on our course. We have two primary modes of anticipation: our anxiety that things will go badly and our hopes that they will go well. The best way to translate either feeling into action is through planning and preparation.

For rock climber Alex Honnold, careful planning and diligent prepa-ration is a matter of life or death. Imagine your life on the line as you stand at the base of a twelve-hundred-foot-tall slab of sandstone towering in front of you. That's the height of the Empire State Building. You take a breath and then grip the wall and begin to climb. Each new hold demands your complete concentration as you ascend higher—poor finger place-ment could mean the difference between climbing and falling. Now imag-ine doing it without ropes, nets, water, food, or any assistance.

That's what Honnold did when he free-soloed the infamous crack climb, Moonlight Buttress, in Zion National Park. His secret? He antici-pated what he would do every inch of the climb before he grabbed his first hold. Honnold wrote, "I had performed all the hard work on Moonlight Buttress during the days leading up to the climb. Once I was on the route, it was just a matter of executing." Bouldering requires intense focus, every sequence of movement planned in advance. Failure to plan can result in an embarrassing fall in a gym—or a lethal one from a cliff.

Plan plan plan. Get into the smallest details. That's how Hercule Poirot, Christie's main protagonist, cracked his cases. Poirot is an older man and retired from the force. He is stuffed with experience and blessed with the patience that can allow us to believe he actually is, as he once explained, "the world's greatest detective." With his remarkable memory and superb eye for the minuscule, Poirot calls on his extensive knowledge of human behavior via his "little gray cells" to solve mysteries deductively. It is for others—like his somewhat clumsy cohort, Hastings—to gather the information on foot that Poirot knows is best excavated while seated in his armchair. Like Jim Thorpe, Poirot is a visualizer.

Even if you are not a world-class athlete or a great detective, you can use visualization as you anticipate and plan for your future. However, please note: both the thrill of excitement we feel in anticipating a happy outcome and the anxiety in contemplating how things might go awry are valuable. The trick is to always prepare for the worst case and also the best.

Let's take the worst case first. Remember that this approach is a powerful energy generator. Christie often steps up the pressure on the reader as her story moves along by introducing the threat of another murder—blood on our hands—if we don't get the culprit NOW. She counts on our very human tendency to imagine the worst.

Perhaps you're like me when you start your day. You hope things will go smoothly but anticipate that they might not. Left unchecked, this can turn into rumination, but if monitored and harnessed, it can be made active. Used correctly, this is realism, not defeatism. And it can become a spark for action. It means we acknowledge the possibility of obstacles—and are ready for them.

In November 2014, I was on an Amtrak train from New York to Washington, D.C. I'd been invited by the Library of Congress to participate in an event honoring Billy Joel with the Gershwin Prize for Popular Song. My contribution was to restage a portion of the 2002 Broadway musical *Movin' Out*, which I'd created around eighteen songs from Billy's catalog. The dancers were well rehearsed. The next day we'd convene at Constitution Hall for a run-through with Billy's band before the real thing that evening. I would also give a short speech about Billy—of whom I am very fond—and return home the next morning. A pleasant forty-eight-hour turnaround. I was looking forward to the celebration. However, when I got off the train, instead of going to my hotel with the group, I directed the driver to Constitution Hall. I wanted to see the stage setup for our part of the program.

The anticipation I felt as we pulled up to the theater was not a tingle of pleasure but a roil of worry. I assumed the stage would be set up to showcase Billy's music, not my dancers. It made sense: it was his night. Still, I believed that as invited participants, we deserved the courtesy of being presented at our best. But sure enough, an array of large loudspeakers had already been arranged at the front of the stage in standard rock-and-roll formation. Good for projecting clear sound but guaranteed to block half of the action onstage. Even from the best seats, people would barely see the dancers' legs and feet. The TV sight lines wouldn't be much better. If I allowed this to go unchallenged, the audience would be laughing at us—hardly the desired effect. It took some strenuous cajoling to fix the problem, but eventually, the producers and stagehands agreed that the speakers could be lowered onto makeshift stands below the front of the stage and quickly returned after we finished.

I am well acquainted with Murphy's Law (if something can go wrong, it will). When we anticipate, we can head Murphy off at the pass. That's why I visited the theater the moment I arrived in town rather than waiting until the next day along with everyone else. By anticipating disaster on day one, I had freed up a moment on day two of the trip to think calmly of my small speech and get a genuine smile from Billy on camera in response.

Your fear of disaster can be translated into action by thinking ahead and addressing the issues you see percolating. But careful: too much cautious anticipation breeds fear, and like anger, fear is dirty fuel. Immerse yourself too often in bleak mode, you'll see nothing but dangers and disasters, and pretty soon you'll want to shuffle off to sit in the corner and pull your hat over your head—by which time it's usually too late to do anything about it. That's no way to move forward. Use your worry, but know when to leave it behind.

The other pathway to counter Murphy's Law is by visualizing success. The next time your brain is crowded with troubling thoughts or you're dreading a future event (a tough meeting, a boring obligation, a painful encounter with relatives), picture a sequence of actions that can make you happy with the outcome. Rehearse them in your mind. Then sleep on it. You're not relying on hope. You're engaging in active anticipation, and your odds of a pleasant experience will be improved dramatically.

Whether you are motivated by your hope for reward or by your fear of pain, thinking things through and preparing allows you to avoid issues before they develop—to discover the culprit before he murders again! You can either put in the extra hours of practice to avoid a bad review, operating under fear, or you can be so cocksure about your great idea that you don't even consider the prospect of failure. Both work.

Anticipation is a skill that needs constant tending. Practice this: each day expect one miracle—one instance of elegance or beauty from the world—it's your right. It doesn't have to be big. Go into the garden each morning to see what has blossomed. Some days improvising a few original steps—the equivalent of a novelist calling it a day after composing one useful sentence—suffices as my miracle. Or it's someone using a word I've never heard before, the miracle being an expanded vocabulary. Or it's finding a hawk nesting in Central Park—a small wonder of nature. Other times it's hearing a Beethoven chord and understanding that I can appropriate his musical form into my dance thinking. I don't need much and I don't know what it will be, but I always expect to find something. So I look for it, which increases the chances of success.

A daily miracle is part of our deal. It's a bad day when I find nothing. I go to bed cranky. The good news is that the disappointment washes away through the night and I wake up renewed, expecting the next miracle all over again.

Y ou may already think you're anticipating well if you start your day with a checklist of things to do. But a to-do list is wishing, not projecting yourself into the future. What if we could codify anticipation, transforming it from a tingly sensation into a repeatable skill? Can each tomorrow be scripted in real life as well as in detective stories? We both know reality isn't as well written as a Christie novel. Plan for digressions but keep the trajectory in mind.

I want you to connect to the full arc of your lifelong pledge, not just your to-do list for tomorrow. It comes down to anticipating the moment when the curtain comes down. Will you have reached a satisfying denouement? A sense that you lived your life as you intended, with meaning?

When I script the day ahead, my mind races through a checklist of challenging questions:

- *Why are you doing this?* In other words, do you care what happens?

- *Where's the conflict?* Every good script has a moment of conflict. With whom will I clash? Where are the pockets of resistance?

- *What is the one response you dread? Or can't afford?* The answer is always indifference and boredom—the vision of people falling asleep or leaving early. It reminds me of the wisest rule of writing from Elmore Leonard: "Try to leave out the part that readers tend to skip." This is pure anticipation.

- *Who is reliable?* A good script needs a hero. Before I enter a situation, I have a sense of who's on my side.

- *What personal biases am I bringing that will defeat me?* I have blind spots and contrarian beliefs. My script needs a reminder to acknowledge them, then bury them.

With script in hand, you can enter a room telling yourself, *I know how this story turns out*, and you will be the hero. Most satisfying, of course, is when you can consider your ending a win/win. People who look beyond themselves to what might please or serve others are the real heroes and deserve all the dopamine coming their way.

Another surefire way to get the dopamine flowing is to share our pleasure with others. We have two choices when we discover something elegant. We can put it in our pocket and keep it to ourselves, or we can share it and gain a higher order of appreciation. In this case, we enjoy anticipating the response of the other. When I finish a piece, before it has premiered, I imagine how the audience will respond—*Will this dance make sense to them? Are they going to laugh? Was that my intention? Will they recognize themselves?* Then looking through the audience's eyes, I inquire, *Is there a spot in the dance where my intention may be weak or confused?* Next I go to work fixing these passages so I can look forward to the premiere, when we will all discover whether there is any truth to be shared in what I have made. Hopefully, pleasure in the maker will become pleasure in the receiver. What more can one ask?

You can make sharing delight into a daily occurrence, not a rare event. The dopamine payoff is merely the bonus that prompts you to do the same the next day and the next, and it works in reverse. Simply ask your friends each time you meet, "What did you learn today?"

DAILY PACT TO SHARE

Make a daily pact with a good friend to share something that you believe will either fascinate or instruct the other. It could be a recipe, a song, an obscure quote, an original thought, a gift, a takeout meal. It can arrive at any time, in person, on the phone, electronically, via home delivery. A physical discovery is particularly attractive—"I walked an extra half mile today and felt great."

The key is that it's a two-way exchange of anticipation—incoming and outgoing. You have created a mutual anticipation society. If daily is too much, settle on one day a week (call it "Wait for It Wednesday" if you wish). You're still anticipating; it just takes longer.

I know: Isn't this why we have Facebook? So friends can update friends with miraculous media sightings? For the purposes of this exercise, let's anticipate on a higher level than one more cat video.

Here's another idea for content: The Daily Miracle. Find something that pleases you greatly first thing every morning when your mind is fresh. Email it to a friend. From my editor: "I went in to work early today and did tour jetés and cabrioles in the hallway. Heaven." Way to go.

Before he passed away in 2015, Richard Burke, composer and star music professor at Hunter College, was an unfailing font of miracles for me. Yes, he was brilliant musically—he played Bach exquisitely—but his energy came from communicating his passion with others. His musical knowledge was bottomless, and he was generous—even philanthropic—with it. He would host me on Sundays at his Upper East Side apartment to fill gaps in my musical erudition. Each visit was devoted to one composer or one moment in music history—a private tutorial while other folks in Manhattan were brunching. One day it would be Schubert's quartets, another day Sibelius's Second Symphony or Grieg's *Lyric Pieces.* He'd play recordings while reviewing the scores, and my ears would open to music that should not have been new to me. For an encore, he'd retreat to his kitchen and return with a marvelous vanilla almond torte or strawberry souffle that he'd baked for the occasion. I always anticipated two miracles—having my musical misconceptions addressed, then dessert—with Richard.

There's no time limit on how near or far into the future our anticipation stretches. We anticipate meeting friends in a few hours, or getting tenure in five years, or paying off our mortgage in thirty years. And we can accommodate all three time horizons simultaneously. Thinking ahead, Agatha Christie wrote *Curtain*, the last of her many Poirot novels, at fifty-five, then buried it in a vault for thirty years before publishing it at age eighty-five. Christie saw it coming—she had anticipated that after a certain age, she wasn't going to be able to write as well as she once had, so she saved *Curtain* to publish a year before her death, assured of closing Poirot on a strong note.

Presumably, our horizons shorten as we get older. We don't project too far forward because we don't know if we'll be around to reap the reward. A morbid thought perhaps, like the age-old joke about not buying green bananas because you might not be around by the time they're ripe. But is it true? Is there a shelf life for anticipating? Do we have less to anticipate as we get older and, therefore, anticipate less frequently?

It depends. What we anticipate for ourselves is a private choice and varies wildly from person to person. Some press on, some change the channel. John Updike was writing poems about his cancer a few weeks before his passing—and still expressed the "irrational hope" that his final book, *Endpoint*, containing those poems would be his best. Frank Sinatra retired several times, building a late career out of comebacks. Tony Bennett is touring in his nineties, still anticipating the next show. Like all great performers, Bennett hones his craft rigorously. And like all great showmen, he loves to entertain, to share what he knows when he gives a show.

Operative here is the word "give."

Like Dinesen in "Babette's Feast," learn to anticipate reward through the impact your choices have on others. Ultimately it is their response—not your efforts—that you will remember.

Chapter Seven

The Long Haul

Exercise 7: Build Your Stamina *page 96*

The test starts in a studio on Manhattan's West Thirty-seventh Street. Twelve dancers are about to set out on an impossible quest. Cue drumroll. At the end of the rehearsal, I ask them to form a circle and join hands with me, look one another in the eye, and pledge, "I will not go down." It is our last run-through before we hit the road with an evening of all new work in celebration of the fiftieth anniversary of my pledge to a life of dance. After the tour we can all collapse, not before.

Dancers are used to difficult classes, grueling rehearsals, and more challenging, a run of performances one night after another, week after week. But taking a show out on the road is another matter completely, a real feat of stamina for all on the bus.

I'll be going out with them—staying in the same hotels, pulling my own bags. Forty-four performances in ten cities over sixty-six days. It would have been tough at twenty-four. At seventy-four, what was I thinking? But this test of my pledge—and of my dancers—is a callout to forces much larger than myself. To music, to our parents, who made sure we could learn to appreciate Bach and New Orleans jazz in the same program, and to our loved ones, who support our efforts on a daily basis. And to the troopers in all our lives, going back millennia to the troubadours and clowns who set out to entertain the world with only the truths they had locked away in their bodies. All these are with us when we get on the tour bus. It's pretty crowded.

Once we are out on the road, drama adds to the burden. Buckled in car or plane seats, air-conditioning blasting, our bodies freeze. The irony is that the speed of modern traveling simultaneously provides one of the fastest ways we have to lose our conditioning. We must constantly remind ourselves to stretch and keep the joints juiced, every morning traveling, every rest stop we get. Stamina fades fast with immobility, and the more tired we become, the more critical it is to confront this reality.

Stamina is exertion maintained over time. It's not only the indefatigability of an ultramarathoner running a hundred-mile race in under twelve hours (averaging seven minutes a mile). It's also the ability to deliver shorter bursts of intense activity more than once or twice a day, then again the next day. I've always gauged my stamina by dividing the day into thirds—the morning for working out, the afternoon for rehearsal, the late afternoon and evening for performances and business dinners. I expect a lot from my stamina: as much energy and alertness at the end of the day as I had at the start.

Chances are, if you are reading this, you feel a need to boost your stamina. Most of us do. As hard as it is to take a first step to rid yourself of complacency, whenever you push outside your comfort zone, you are at least rewarded with a sense of accomplishment for making that first move. However, the real effort comes not in getting started but in continuing forward after the flush of newness has faded.

When we drive ourselves forward, our bodies adapt. When we don't push, our bodies idle, then stagnate, lolling in their comfort zone. Adaptation is a great benefit, but we must work to get there. It's why my trainer adds more weight to the bar when three sets of fifteen reps at the old weight no longer challenges me. I go back to eight reps at a greater weight and over several sessions work up to fifteen. Then he repeats the cycle with a little more weight. That is the reward. It is also how our muscles strengthen.

It's the same in any process of continuous improvement, whether we're trying to extend our attention span or tighten our abs. You have to gradually challenge yourself to do a little more each day, or you're wasting your time. If you've been doing the same hundred sit-ups a day for the last ten years, you lost most of the improvement benefit after the first few weeks. It may feel like losing ground to struggle with a new challenge, but it's really the only way to go forward. Goals must be constantly refreshed. Any good trainer will remind you when you are getting complacent. (And here's a secret: you can do a few more reps of anything.)

You've got to internalize this. Start by becoming your own trainer. Even though we love our trainers and they set the gold standard for our exercise discipline, there comes the time when you have to hold your own feet to the fire, counting the number of reps, watching the clock, keeping the sets moving. Even with the consistency of regular performances, my dancers and I still must maintain our own training routines, same as it ever was, over and over. While on tour, finding a gym in every town helps us maintain our pledge. Some of the gyms are less than ideal—machines dangerously out of order, stained green plastic rugs, the occasional roach. No matter, our stamina builds rather than decreases with the consistent work.

The idea is to set goals that are reasonable enough that you can accomplish them, acknowledge the success, and then start on the new goal. Enough of these and you can reward yourself by imagining even bigger challenges. The crucial element here is that you continue to push. And it can be a small push. But without making forward progress—trying to run a faster sprint, refining your elevator pitch, being more connected to your spouse—time evaporates without value.

By Bloomington, Indiana, halfway through the journey, we all understand why one wag calls this tour "The Bataan Death March." By now the dancers are tired and dancing on automatic, their performance becoming rote. This must be addressed. Whenever I have tough news to deliver, there will be a company dinner, so in Bloomington, our forty-sixth day on the road, I schedule one of my you-know-what-is-coming dinners.

After orders are taken, I begin. "Guys, you've gotten too good." (I always try to bring bad news in a pleasant way.) "You're getting boring."

Part of stamina is staying focused, but having to perform something over and over risks the body—and the brain—going numb. I ask my troupe to wake up to their now and give me a fresh show. And I remind them there is another kind of repetition, one with a different challenge than simply stamina.

I once lived next door to master harpsichordist Rosalyn Tureck. Listening to her practice difficult passages in Bach's music over and over was to marvel at the ingenuity of a great performer bringing to bear many different approaches and intentions to the repetition of the same bars of canonic music. Each pass accomplished a different goal. Creative repetition teaches us there is no single right way.

Yes, you have to fight through walls to build stamina and this tour's hardships offer plenty. But you don't quit taking a test because you don't know one answer and you don't settle on last night's show as the be-all and end-all of tonight's. New ways must be found in every performance and pushing through to the next and the next gives you more options for passing future tests.

While many of our physical tools diminish noticeably as we age—speed, flexibility, and power—we don't have to lose stamina. The more my youthful powers wane, the more I appreciate stamina as the great equalizer. If we have stamina, we can keep going no matter what the clocks and calendars show. That said, the fact that we have the capacity to retain our stamina well into old age doesn't guarantee we will actually do it. Stamina is a choice, not a birthright. We develop it over time by practicing simple steps—and repeating them.

Hua Chi, a Buddhist monk in China now in his seventies, has repeated the same ritual for fifty years. Every day before sunrise, he goes to temple. Once there, he bends down to pray in the same spot. He then rises and repeats his activity, his action similar to what we would call a squat thrust. Over and over, an unbelievable three thousand times every single morning. This ritual has created a physical artifact: the imprint of his footprints ingrained in the temple's wood floor. With stamina to burn, he looks like he could live to be a thousand. Hard work keeps his aging from getting old.

I don't gauge time through clocks and calendars. I measure time with my body. When I breathe in and out, or hear my heart beating, or shift from one foot to the other, I sense the passing of time. When nothing moves, I lose that sense. In the same way that a sundial measures time through solar movement and an hourglass does the same with falling sand, my body has become my clock—because it moves. I know time through movement.

At the start of our lives, we believe time stretches into infinity, despite the evidence of mortality all around us. Time feels abundant, inexhaustible, impossible to measure. When I was young, my time frame was forever. Why not? When you're just beginning, why stunt the experience by worrying about how it ends? Still deep into my seventies, I refuse to think of time draining away.

If we can move, we can measure time. A literal measurement is the time step. For example, a great tap dancer like Honi Coles or Greg Hines held a short four-beat phrase steady—not losing time—for hours. You become the clock, you are time.

┌─── BUILD YOUR STAMINA ───

What physical activity does your body know as a unit of time? Maybe taking the stairs at work or walking the dog ten minutes around the block is a unit for you. My grandson's karate kick-flip-thwonk is his measure of a second. The heart beating, the breath in and out. All of these measure your life passing in time.

Take your small unit—could be a push-up, could be a goose step, could be a bend to the right and then to the left. Breathe in on the preparation, breathe out on the work. Now repeat. Each repetition is a victory. Keep count.

Enlarge your numbers daily. That is how we build stamina.

Training muscles rigorously means that the repetitions need to be as close to identical as possible. Watch any great runner. You will see a stride that has been honed to the most efficient transfer of weight from foot to foot. And then repeated. Millions of times. Muscles train best by moving in a single path. You can't train them if they're wandering around.

Set a number of repetitions for your unit and picture a culmination for your stamina to realize. At least five repeats in your building's stairwell. Or ten in the shower before you turn on the water. Take on the challenge. When you have accomplished it, celebrate—and then set a new goal. Enough of these and you can reward yourself by imagining more and greater challenges. As we say in the gym, more weight is your reward.

For the truly advanced, hell-bent on maximal stamina, there is the rope. For building stamina it is par excellence. Boxers jump nine minutes or the equivalent of three rounds continuously without rest. Assuming you cannot do three rounds, start with one minute on and rest thirty seconds for three sets as your goal. Then work your way up. Whenever a dancer needs to build stamina coming back from an injury, it is the jump rope that is the most efficient training. The tedium becomes as grueling as the physical work. So be creative—vary speed, footwork, and arm placement as you swing the rope. Skip some, hop some, two-feet some. Slow meter, double time, at the speed of a blur. When you can work up to three minutes on, rest for thirty seconds and build up to ten sets, you will be in shape.

And the reward? Over the long haul, stamina builds to endurance. *Sisu* is a Finnish word that means a perseverance bordering on stubbornness, staying the course with determination and direction. The word is derived from *sisus*, which translates to "guts." This makes an intuitive sort of sense to me because it is your gut that transforms fuel into the energy for movement. Endurance is a combination of willpower, focus, intention, and grit—essentially a matter of character and mental toughness.

Jiro Ono wakes up every morning and goes to work in his Tokyo restaurant, Sukiyabashi Jiro. Ono is in his late eighties, long past the age when most people have decided to quit working. He seems to be allergic to rest. Sukiyabashi Jiro has only ten seats, no restroom, and serves only one thing: sushi. No appetizers, no desserts, no side dishes. Just sushi. And yet this modest establishment has earned a coveted three stars from Michelin. Ono never settles. His ceaseless dedication to one activity might give you the impression of a life lived in the comfort zone, but in fact, it is just the opposite. He is the essence of vitality as he relentlessly pursues perfection each day—the ideal consistency for his rice, the perfect crispness of the nori, the very freshest and most flavorful fish. After decades of being in business, he increased the amount of time his chefs massage the octopus from thirty to fifty minutes, simply because he had learned it would improve the tenderness. Ono only closes the restaurant on holidays, coming in every day to devote himself to pleasing his customers. This is his pledge, reflecting his stamina, endurance, and grit.

The culmination of our dance tour and our test comes when we return to New York City. It is eight weeks after we began and we are finally sleeping in our own beds. We will finish the tour beginning week nine with seven performances in six days at one of dance's most prestigious venues, the Koch Theater at Lincoln Center. Now in the homestretch, we are all tired but keyed up to premier these dances in our hometown.

I sit in the orchestra on the first night with Brady, my tour manager, seated to my right. The seats around us are intentionally empty because adjacency is dangerous. I am never a passive audience. My feet keep count. My head bobs and shakes. When I see something irksome, I elbow Brady, who notes the specific moment for discussion with the company later. An off night can be bruising for him.

And opening night is off. Some of it is nerves. The dancers, so eager to show well, are pushing, trying too hard. But under the circumstances, I'd have been surprised if they weren't a little on edge.

What really concerns me is their stamina. They are weary from two months on the road and performing at Lincoln Center gives the whole enterprise a do-or-die vibe. I watch as they dig deep.

But the next night is no better. Nor the next. Three B to B+ performances in a row. I fear that the dancers have hit the wall—and that the tour's final four performances will be a quiet denouement instead of a triumphant hurrah.

Then before the curtain goes up on Friday, I'm watching them warm up as usual. I'm stunned to see that they're fresher than ever. It's in their eyes and their legs, all crackle and precision and attack. They haven't lost their stamina. They've found a second wind.

I'm thinking, *What's happening here? This is going to be a really strong show.* And so it is. Their fortieth performance is their strongest yet. And they get stronger on Saturday. By Sunday's matinee, like a miler delivering a devastating finishing kick, they have widened the gap between all other shows. Their last performance is miraculous.

This is the dancers' heavenly reward for adhering with monklike devotion to their routines. As the tour ends and reaches the last show, we are assured that no one is going down. The pledge has protected us. Now tossing caution aside, the dancers dig even deeper and bring up their absolute best.

That's the wonderful thing about stamina: it doesn't deplete through a long period of grinding work; with sustained commitment, it builds and builds, up to the moment when you need it most. The end.

Chapter Eight

Bounce Back

Exercise 8: Squirm *Page 108*

D on't look in his eyes—stay focused on the target." These were Teddy Atlas's instructions to boxer Michael Moorer, going into the ring to defend his 1994 heavyweight title. The challenger was George Foreman. Foreman's odds of winning at age forty-five were—according to one of the announcers—"a gazillion to one." Foreman came out at the bell and went straight to the center. There he set up shop. Moorer, not listening to his coach to go right, managed to open a cut over Foreman's left eye and kept going for it.

Foreman, however, had Angelo Dundee—the best cut man in the business—coaching in his corner. Because Foreman, at 6′4″, refused to sit between rounds, Dundee had difficulty reaching up to the eye, but he still managed to tell Big George, going into the tenth round, now was the time to finish the job. George did so, a classic right to the jaw, and then left the ring at 45 years and 360 days, the oldest man to gain the heavyweight title on record. The only man to defeat an opponent nineteen years his junior and the only man to win the heavyweight title after losing it twenty years before. (That loss, in one of the all-time great fights, the Rumble in the Jungle 1974 in Zaire, was to Muhammad Ali.)

I took singular interest in Foreman's 1994 comeback fight because Teddy had once been my trainer for about six months in 1983 when I was attempting a comeback fight of my own.

Resilience goes by many names. Educators prize it as *grit*, commanding officers inculcate it as *endurance*, my weight trainer measures it in terms of *recovery time*. I prefer the term *bounce back*, which I share with professional golf. It's how golfers measure their ability to forget a ruinous shot and move on. Bounce back. I like its unambiguous candor. You get knocked down, you bounce back up. In my personal hierarchy of techniques to keep you from stalling out as the years go by, bounce back is the essential skill—numero uno.

In a long life, patterns emerge. For most of us, our lives assume the ebb and flow of a sine wave. No matter how doggedly we move forward, or how thoroughly we anticipate the future, there will be blows to bring us low from time to time. We need to absorb the impact and move not just forward but out of a trough and on to a crest. Stopped dead by a blow? Not if you have resilience to keep you moving along.

Here are six thoughts to help you acquire the resilience you will need for your inevitable comebacks.

1. Get Past Imposter Syndrome

When we are down for the count, it's easy to become intimidated. In its most extreme, this dashed confidence can balloon into full-fledged imposter syndrome. We don't see a mistake or lessons to learn. We see a character flaw. We feel like a fraud, question our talent, our intentions, certain that others, too, see through our charade, afraid that we will never be accepted again. And if some of our critics are of this mind, we listen to them rather than to our better angels because we are tired. Because we just lost.

During the Ali fight, at the receiving end of a crazy fight crowd yelling, "Kill the bum," Foreman was knocked out for the first time ever in his career. He simply couldn't recognize himself as a loser and he quit the ring for several years.

I, too, have had my moments. At forty-five, I'd been mostly directing and making dances for others for ten years and found myself woefully out of shape. I had begun to wonder if I would ever be able to really dance again myself. Dancing was my shield. Without it and reviewed on the performance of others, I felt disoriented by criticism. How had I allowed this to happen? As I aged, I was beginning to see my own steps stronger on other bodies and I started feeling more than a bit fraudulent in the studio. I was used to jumping higher than everyone else, going longer or faster than humanly possible. That was how I knew to control the room. Now I was going to have to find another way.

I entered a depression of major proportions, retreating into a corner of self-pity and confusion. In desperation, I took up Nobody's alternative and just skipped town. *Escaping to a new place can help us gain new perspectives*, I told myself. *New horizon, new time zone, new you.*

Without announcing my plans to anyone, I exiled myself to Los Angeles. I checked in to a funky hotel in a residential section of West Hollywood, no doubt because I associate being down and out with that town's desiccated landscape. If I wanted to flagellate myself, Los Angeles was where I had to be.

I found an idle church nearby and convinced the management to let me use some basement space as a dance studio. I forced myself to go in to work every day for at least three hours. I needed to return to hard work in the studio to feel physically powerful again, the best way I know to recapture some self-respect. This exercise was not going to be pretty, but at least it would be something. I reminded myself to do the work on the inhale and release on the exhale. Then I started building from the bottom up.

Watch any fighters when knocked down and on their backs. Their movement is small as they struggle to get traction and wriggle to their knees, then their feet. I call it a squirm. First thing on a really bad morning, flat on your back—wishing the ref would just get past ten already—you can practice it, too.

SQUIRM

Down and out, go to our common evolutionary beginning and *squirm*. A wriggling moment—squirming looks like what it sounds like—a worm moving. It is formless physical effort, the vaguest of movement inside your skin.

Picture this in your mind now and move in your chair. Then, before you have to look in the mirror tomorrow morning, you will try it in your bed for real. Lying on your back, move your torso to the right, then the left, then back to the right. Next, bend the legs slightly. Now bend the legs again while flexing those feet—feel the stretch in the back of your heels. Don't forget to breathe.

Now arch the back. Arch again and roll the upper shoulders back. Release. In bed, with repetitions, you will travel ever so slightly, but that is not the point. Starting is the point.

Now roll onto your stomach. This next is the inverse of the arch you just completed: contract the abs so they are pulling you in and curve the back out. As you release, push in to the bed with your toes.

Again on your back, raise your hands—shake them. Jaw—move it from side to side. Scowl. Release. Forearms wave back and forth. If you can, try flowing in what you might imagine as a Hawaiian greeting from the shoulders. Still on the bed, breathe deeply, now add shoulder rolls back. Roll to your right side and stretch the left leg across. Reverse that. Now start getting up from the bed. Double over in the direction of your feet and stand up.

Feeling better but not quite ready to go? Focus on the breath—in for a count of four, hold for four, exhale for four, hold for four. Ten of these deep breaths should make a difference. Now you should be ready to start your day. Your whole day will be stronger for having taken the time to wake up your body before you demand that it get to work.

None of this may seem that challenging, but think of it as your better-than-nothing workout.

That's how I began the L.A. days. The bed beginning gave me purchase, when I got to the church, to pick up where I left off the day before and I worked to strengthen my base every day. Still, there are those days when that is not going to happen. So just acknowledge a slow day. But not a worthless one. Pace yourself accordingly and try to be patient. The important thing is to start somewhere.

Day by day, move by move, practice who you are and where you are at that very moment. Being connected to your body in its current state will allow you to be more realistic about what you need next, both in your day and in your bounce back.

Enlarging on the confidence of your squirm, you can start asking questions. Are you still extrapolating from one old event to find a condemnation of your talent, determination, or smarts?

You miss a deadline and conclude, therefore, *I am an irresponsible employee.* Can it not simply be:

I missed a deadline; I need to learn to manage time better and set more reasonable goals.

I've never met someone who did not feel this way on occasion. When you encounter a setback or criticism, ask yourself: *What really happened? How would I describe this event if it had happened to someone else?* You'll likely find that imagining another person in the screwup allows you to be more compassionate and logical. *How big a deal is this, anyway? What was at stake? Is it irrevocable?*

Meanwhile, keep the squirm moving and pushing your momentum forward.

2. Framing

In a comeback, you must train your mind to find what's useful in any difficult situation. From childhood, William Faulkner was passionate about riding horses. He fell often. When he was recovering in bed from a painful spill, someone asked, "Why do you keep getting back on horses?" He replied, "Because it's the best training for writing." He framed his falling as an education. Brilliant.

That which was negative becomes positive. Find your strongest feature and go with it. Then you can start to zero in on what you can take away from your fall.

Dancers have a wonderful device for accomplishing new framing: a mirror. When they fear they are not reaching their potential—their pliés not deep enough, their leaps not high enough, their transitions muddy or uncertain—watching their performance in a mirror allows them to step away from their own subjective experience. A mirror doesn't have an opinion. Used objectively, the mirror helps the dancer make adjustments as the image in the mirror becomes he or she, not me.

There's nothing that facilitates finding the right frame quite like imagining a situation from someone else's point of view. Looking at it through their eyes, without the muddle of hurt feelings and other negative emotions clouding up the lens, can give you a clear-eyed sense of your reaction to a setback. After a hitch in the road—a negative performance review, a child behaving badly, a project that falls through—take note of your response as if watching from a distance. Is your initial reaction to catastrophize? Once he began his comeback, Foreman reflected back, used his sparring partners' eyes as his mirror. He saw that he could still promote terror. Thus Teddy's admonition—"Don't look in his eyes"—to Moorer going into the fight.

But after we terrorize ourselves with self-doubt, our only relief is to get moving again. Foreman found the grit to begin over and start the training and preliminary fights necessary to get his title shot. During exhibition fights, he began to see himself as a winner, not as he had been going into the Manila fight, but as he was now, slower, less power in his punches. But smarter. He had always been a stand-and-punch kind of fighter. With stamina and now much, much smarter, he was a different fighter but still a winner.

3. Get with the Better Program

Now that you see more clearly what happened, find the lesson. Do the work. Look at your mistake, figure out what you did wrong, and fix it for next time. Find changes to make, however small or incremental. Maybe you wake up earlier in the morning, or alter your evening routine, or choose a different friend to call on for sound counsel.

For myself, when bouncing back in L.A., I zeroed in on why I hadn't been getting the results I needed when demonstrating to my performers. How had I been communicating to my dancers? With tentative moves. Find a new way. Use language. I remembered learning falls in class with Martha Graham when she was in her seventies. She did not attempt to show us. She sat on the low Noguchi bench and inspired us with language to execute her movement. We were elevated by her inspiration.

When I talked to people, it wasn't as if I panicked with stage fright. I'd given many lectures, getting by on whimsy and charm. But I was a show-don't-tell girl, so words were a second, not a first, language for me. I was going to have to work on this.

So, I signed on for a monologue class near the UCLA campus, standing up in front of a roomful of actors and slowly learning how to speak in front of strangers. To deliver a monologue well, you must shape it with specific intention and character, and this you must first articulate to yourself. The class taught me how to seize control verbally in any situation—to know what I wanted and how to say it, to be able to speak in language as well as I could in movement. I learned that even the slightest adjustments in words or action can make a difference and help you do better. I began to believe in my skills as a verbal communicator.

4. Can't Build a Cathedral? Build a Bridge

Note I said "do it better," not "do it best." You will get old, cold, and stale if you only accept a perfect, triumphant comeback. Remember, the perfect is the enemy of the good. I rank my dances into three buckets of achievement.

First, there are the Ur pieces, the breakthroughs that exhibit a seamless union of intention and result. They don't happen often—maybe a dozen times in more than 160 attempts—but I treasure them. Next are the two or three dozen works that have aged well and are still performed by other companies. That leaves well over one hundred dances. These are my "bridge" works, the pieces I did while I was groping for a breakthrough or attempting to bounce back. Some of them are clearly transitional pieces, showing minuscule progress from one to the next. Some are placeholders, works to fulfill an obligation or fill out a program. These lesser pieces are as important as the more durable work because they connect me from one effort to the next until the day something wonderful materializes. They keep me going. When I can't build a cathedral, I build a bridge to get there.

Bridging is our reminder that we don't have to swing for the fences every time out. It's okay to adjust our aim once in a while. This may not be a comforting admission. Who among us intentionally shoots for the second tier? But over time, it's a required survival skill as we climb back from a flop.

5. Motivation

While you plot your ascent, be sure to look closely at what motivates you. The most easily made error in a bounce back is doing something for the wrong reason. Sometimes our good souls are overcome by the bad judgment called revenge. In one particularly dark period of recovery, I spent months choreographing a piece as an act of revenge on a nemesis. The audience couldn't detect my malign motive in the dancing, but I knew it was there—and it wasn't particularly healing. "A man that studieth revenge," said Francis Bacon, "keeps his own wounds green." (Still, if you find yourself in the throes, use it. At least the dance is good.)

You may be familiar with such an impulse. You're down and out, eager to recover what you feel has been taken from you—your status, good name, self-worth, whatever. You crave vindication. So you allow your resilience to be fueled by overheated "I'll show them" emotion. It's energizing but rarely satisfying. After scaling this new summit, you don't want to feel empty, wondering, "Is that all there is?"

The ultimate purpose of bouncing back is not to repay the world with your scorn. It's to launch yourself into a better position, a higher perch. There is a legend that, going into the Foreman/Ali fight in Zaire, Angelo Dundee—Ali's coach then—managed to get the ring ropes loosened. A knockout is a knockout, but still, this gave Ali, older than Big George by seven years and out of the ring a number of years for refusing the draft, a real advantage. Now much slower than he once was, Ali essentially fought this fight with his back to the rope. The loosened rope made it easier for him to wiggle out of Foreman's reach and when Big George did get to him, it was easier for Ali to absorb Foreman's power. Note: for his title comeback fight in 1994, George had Dundee in his corner. Foreman bore no grudges. And Foreman had earned Dundee's respect with what he had accomplished in his drive back to the top. They made a winning team.

Your bounce back should be initiated by your authentic desire to improve. This is your cue to zoom back into your own perspective. Only you can know what you really want. Only you know how to align your actions with your pledge. The pledge is your bedrock, the ocean floor that allows the waves in your sine curve to ebb and flow. It is consistency. It is daily practice. Plugging along is what gives us the chops to finally ascend.

Like Ali's, it was Foreman's will, not his slowed body, that was unstoppable. Foreman had become an evangelist in his interval of retirement and his natural inclination to win was now fortified by the power of God. And by age. Although many thought his decision to return to the ring was a mistake, Foreman countered that he had returned to prove that age was not a barrier to people achieving their goals. He wanted to show that age forty is not a "death sentence." Also having a force bigger than yourself in the corner helps any fighter.

6. Gaining Closure

Finally, our efforts gather focus, and we make a leap forward, leaving the error behind. One cycle ends and a new one begins. And it feels earned. We recognize this because our audience and our loved ones tell us it is so.

In his comeback fight, Foreman felt he could get the crowd behind him, and he did in the beginning of the tenth round. Teddy Atlas had also warned Moorer about this strategy during the break. Taking strength from the crowd's response to a particularly hard right to Moorer's midsection, Foreman brought it home at the end of the tenth. Then, throwing one brief glance down at Moorer, followed by one briefly up to the sky, Foreman went to a neutral corner and knelt in prayer. The crowd was on their feet, yelling their support.

As for me, I was able to get back to NYC with new skills for communicating. But it wasn't only the monologue class. I was now more comfortable moving in my own skin. I was also able to better talk to the performers about our goals. Do what I say, not what I do.

Soon I guilted Teddy Atlas into "training a girl" and even returned to performing in the eighties for the Olympics in L.A. While the work I made on this occasion was still a physically grueling piece—called *Fait Accompli*—it was what I could do then and not before. The dancing was different, the product of a body older yet now in a new prime and with a reason to keep going—namely to find what might be next.

This is closure. We all crave it. Why is it so hard to get there? Why are we so bad at letting things go? Whether it's ending a phone conversation or concluding a troubled friendship that's well past its sell-by date, or delaying a project because we're nervous about its reception when we finish, we all suffer from closure-phobia.

Artists deal with closure by adhering to the ground rules—the resolving cadence, a lyric's last line, a story's *denouement*—all strategies for a graceful ending.

Extending these criteria into deeper matters of the heart—such as romance and family ties—may seem a reach, but we're already doing it in some cases. When we judge how a date balances talking and listening with us or how quickly our calls are returned, we're establishing rules for initiating closure. It's the same when we tell ourselves to leave the room if Uncle Phil starts talking politics at a family get-together; we're rehearsing the act of letting go around Phil. So why not formalize the criteria—spell out what is not acceptable and make closure easy on ourselves?

A simple practice for beginners: pick one thing to drop this week. It could be sugar in your coffee, a long-running argument with your spouse, an unfinished book that's boring you, a nagging criticism that keeps rattling around your skull. Select it, delete it, take your pulse. Why did you make this particular choice? What were your ground rules? Sugar is killing you, the tension at home after spousal battle is unbearable, a dull book steals precious time, the criticism has outlived its usefulness? Stop and take a step forward.

Just as you should expect troughs in your sine wave so too you should expect peaks.

What goes up comes down, what goes around comes around. But hold on, is it only endless bounce back through the sine waves of our lives? What of balance, a center that can hold between the extremes?

Sometimes it is a long time in the coming.

Take Gian Lorenzo Bernini. The leading sculptor and architect of the Baroque era, he was born in Naples in 1598 and is credited with creating a unity in the visual arts not attained by even the great Renaissance artists. He was quoted at the age of sixty-seven saying that, when he was a boy of just six, he had carved a marble head in his father's workshop; scholars have ever since labeled the artist a raving egomaniac desperate to establish his own genius. He was perceived as an old man inflating his ego with the bravado of early precociousness.

To the rescue, my friends the scholars Irving and Marilyn Lavin (who poked each other first thing in the morning in Chapter Four). In 1967 Irving had been introduced to an unidentified seventeenth-century portrait bust which he bought shortly after at auction. For the next fifty years, this mysterious gentleman lived with Irving and Marilyn in their Princeton home. Gradually, Irving had a hunch that this bust was someone with whom he was familiar.

Through some brilliant art historian sleuthing, he first identified the sitter as an Italian magistrate named Farinacci, and then proved this bust an original work by Bernini himself. Irving and Marilyn then developed a grid of Bernini's work and set their bust into its provenance, proving that Bernini had created this masterwork well before the age of twenty. Thus the Lavins validated Bernini's simple recollection of his childhood abilities and cleared away doubts that had clouded the artist's character for centuries.

Justice takes time. In this case 350 years. Call it coincidence or kismet, it is the centering of the scale held by the Roman goddess Iustitia that brings balance to the ups and downs of our sine curves. This balance is called Peace, and it is the final resting place for bounce back. To attain it, we must practice daily. All of it—getting started, blasting out, planning and pacing wisely, having the physical strength and the moral fortitude to keep going when nothing seems in our favor. To relish your highs and weather your lows, get up in the morning with Marilyn's poke, acknowledge you are still alive, and move 'em out. Over and over. Time and again.

Chapter Nine

The Swap

Exercise: To Be a Mortal, Sound Off *Page 127*

everal years ago in Atlanta, I was rehearsing an adorable group of children, ages five to ten, all talented and motivated. The children wore Crocs, part of the costume for a new ballet. I was dressed in my usual white shirt, jeans, and running shoes. With grown-up dancers, I can talk through the steps, but children prefer show to tell, so I obliged with a demonstration. As I got up on the toe of my sneaker—a position I'd taken thousands of times before—my foot collapsed to the side, releasing my full weight down through the leg and cracking the metatarsal.

This was a fairly common, unremarkable incident really, except I was sixty-nine years old and this was the first major injury of my career. Until that moment, I'd never done bodily harm to myself. Never twisted an ankle or torn a muscle or broken a bone. An impressive winning streak, only some of which I attribute to luck.

Perhaps something like this has happened to you. Your moment probably looked different: you reached for a book on a high shelf and felt a sharp twinge in your back. You wrestled with a tightly screwed jar and, in defeat, asked stronger hands to open it. You hesitated before jumping down from a high stool at a restaurant, worried about the shock to your knees, then chose a safer route back to earth. If so, you appreciate the significance of that first moment when your body breaks its contract with you. You can no longer entertain the illusion that you are among the immortals, those who throw themselves delightedly after perfection with childlike intensity because they can. You begin to morph into a mere mortal.

You may not have even realized you were under the illusion of being an immortal, but while mortality can appear at thirty, forty, or fifty, be assured it happens to us all sooner or later. It is the moment when you start to doubt whether you have control over your body after all. You resign yourself to aging.

This new reality is a particular blow to the dancer. Dancers are trained to accomplish the near impossible with ease. They are Olympians, their perfected artistry guaranteeing immortality until one day their body talks back. Age erodes everything the dancer has worked to be since childhood. This is a betrayal not only of the body but of belief and dreams and income and it demands to be dealt with. And by us all, whether dancer or not.

At sixty-nine, I had been staving off the inevitable for decades, understanding well that if you maintain one physical discipline for a lifetime, your body will wear out. Using the same joints, the same muscles, in the same way for ages taxes them. It makes more sense to move the stress around. Over time the trick, I'd discovered, was to measure success through the challenge in front of me, not the one I faced two or twenty years earlier.

As we change, so, too, must our regimens. Looking back over my life, I can identify an evolution in the conditioning strategies I employed as each decade passed. Here's what it looked like for me.

My twenties were basically heaven. Ask it and I did it—across the board in classes, performances, rehearsals. My stamina was beyond. Flexibility, yeah. Speed was a specialty. Power, actually not as great as it would become later. My coordination let me flip movement in space, over under forward back, torso going counter or parallel to the hips. Isolations were honed to where I could deliver movement off a single muscle. I was a big jumper. My falls were fearless. Balance was always my weakness, but you would never know. Eating was anything, any time. My body was tireless— there was no such thing as fatigue, just the extreme pleasure and excitement of moving through space.

In my thirties, I maintained this total focus on my physical instrument even as the responsibilities of adulthood increased. I had a son to care for. I took on a home in Manhattan. I had a company of dancers to manage. I was performing more frequently, sometimes more than a hundred days a year. These were all good things, but with dwindling hours to maintain my usual regimen, I shortened my workouts and increased their intensity. I called it "blasting" because it required explosive energy—and like an explosion, it didn't last long. I'd go all out for eight or nine minutes at first, eventually sustaining thirty minutes of hard aerobic nonstop improvising. Then I'd rest for five or ten minutes and do it again. After an hour, I'd be drenched in sweat and done with my physical work for the day.

In my forties, I was dancing less, managing more. I began to work in the conditioning arena—floor stretches, still a ballet barre daily—I became careful about what I ate. I started using the Canadian air force exercises, doubling down on squat thrusts, push-ups, jumping jacks. I also began boxing under the amused eye of trainer Teddy Atlas. I loved the speed bag, did okay running flights of stairs backward, was good on the rope, and hated getting hit. I focused on endurance.

In my fifties, I stopped training as a dancer and started lifting weights. I had no interest in becoming one of the "ancients" at the back of the room in a ballet class, straining my body beyond what was healthy simply because it was what I had always known. It was time for something more appropriate. Because I was no longer performing, fitness became its own reward. I had a foundation of flexibility, coordination, and speed from the dancing years. I continued daily studio improvising but felt I needed strength, which lifting weights provided, so I focused there. At my peak, I benched my body weight for three reps and could deadlift 225 pounds.

In my sixties, time felt really short and my energy was no longer a bottomless well. I had to be parsimonious with both: so much for me, so much for others. Weight training became the mainstay of my regimen. Improvising dropped off, though for the lead role in *Movin' Out*, the Billy Joel musical, I still built much of the material for the lead role, Eddie, on myself. I remained strong. I measured my success against what I could do, not against the other folks in the weight room.

One of the benefits of choosing a physical life was that from the beginning, I had the sense of body work as an investment. Throughout each decade, I worked not only for the present but to lay down a foundation for the future.

When Warren Buffett said, "My wealth has come from a combination of living in America, some lucky genes, and compound interest," he was shining a light on the wonders of compounding. It is the simplest of economic principles. Let's say you are lucky to have some capital when you're young, and you put away $10,000 in a bank account paying 5 percent interest when you turn twenty-one. Contribute $5,000 a year to the account, and fifty years later, your $260,000 investment will have quintupled into $1.2 million. You can do something similar with your fitness—work hard now to reap greater rewards in the future instead of finding yourself in a panic at your dwindling account. Starting early and distributing the burden throughout my body by engaging in disciplines from ballet to boxing had kept me strong and healthy into my late sixties.

So yes, start early and work with what you've got. But what about that inevitable moment of betrayal? It took until I was sixty-nine and injured in Atlanta to question myself. What new training regimen might I move into now that I, too, had clearly entered mortaldom? I would have to push through self-doubt: *Wait—I'm not going to be perfect? Or at least better than I've ever been before?* With mortality comes a license to make noise. Go ahead and scream.

TO BE A MORTAL, SOUND OFF

Immortals feel no pain, make no great physical effort, and never cry out as they move. Dancers—like immortals—generate the illusion that there is no pain in their efforts, only ease.

But mortals make noise. As you practice these simple isometric stretches, sound off! As you exercise, you are allowed to grunt, squeal, cry. Sound off.

First: put your palms together and stretch the arms straight up from the shoulders. Use these long arms to stir the torso first clockwise, then counterclockwise. Express your deeper feelings. Go ahead.

Now reach laterally—right, then left. Feel the obliques to the left of the torso as you reach right, then reverse. How are they today? Massive GRRR.

Finally, arch back and then forward. With each repetition, increase the depth. Arch back, breathe in, then arch forward, breathe out.

A fun thought: during the day when you have something—anything— you wish to say, stand up and illustrate it with a movement— any movement—of your choice. Jut a hip out to the right, pull up the left knee and slap it with the right hand. Give physical emphasis to all the points you need to make.

And I remind you again that you are a mortal in movement and that for you, screaming is okay.

As we get older, pain is not just a possibility. It is a given one way or another. The dancer learns early to take pain for granted and that there is great freedom in choosing how to respond to its appearance. The thing NOT to do is deny pain. It must be acknowledged. Sometimes the right way of moving forward will be to push through pain. Your choices determine who you will be, who the world will see—someone who is defeated or an adaptive striver.

There are three kinds of athletic pain: challenging pain, warning pain, chronic pain—and countless ways to respond to each, some helpful, others doomed to make you miserable.

Challenging pain is the beneficial unpleasantness of breaking through a fitness barrier—the scorching lungs and muscles when you take the final fifty yards at top speed, eager to "feel the burn." Blasting is challenging pain.

Warning pain is the sharp twinge, tear, pop, or ache that signals you're doing something wrong. Best stop doing it.

Chronic pain is all the stuff—the torn muscle, the bone spur, the hip that needs replacement—you have to tolerate either because there's no fix or because you resist surgical intervention. Chronic pain is not going away, but it's not an excuse to give up.

You can start a pain journal to chronicle your experiences of pain and how you react. Is your pain chronic, blasting, warning? How do you respond to each type when it appears? Do you work through it? Does that help? Do you allow it to stop you from doing things you love? Or are you taking more risks than is advisable? Is it time to see a doctor? Will it be time to start working with a physical therapist? Whichever, embrace your condition and get on with your new program. Use the knowledge you've gathered through experiencing adversity—whether it's how to avoid experiencing more pain or how to respond with spirit and intention when it presents itself again—but do not squander your experience. Skin is tougher when you are scarred, and when you have learned how to right yourself again and again, you become harder to knock off-balance in the future.

Pain brings a great reservoir of information. Part of grappling with your mortality is figuring out how to live with your pain—both physical and emotional—without making your pain the whole of your life. How do you do it? In the most difficult circumstances, sometimes you simply live through it.

I have a chronic injury to my rotator cuff, acquired in my fifties. Twenty years later, it still flares up. But it's not a weight-bearing injury, has never cost a missed performance, never affected my work, so I endure it and move on. Like a soccer player with a broken finger, I regard it as an annoyance, not an injury—something to work around.

I tore the rotator cuff on tour with Baryshnikov in 1992. Misha was dancing on two damaged knees, so we had made a pact to each another (by now you are familiar with my pacts) that neither of us would miss a show in our twenty-two cities. He had his pain and I had mine and we worked through it.

Then the worst happened. My mother, ill, went into the hospital. Between shows, I flew out to meet my two siblings at her bedside. We had to make a decision. My mother did not want to be kept alive artificially. It was gutting, but we respected her wishes.

And I was back on tour the next time the curtain came up. One thing about my mother: she would not have wanted me to miss a show. Of course, to carry on that quickly is extreme. It is not the choice for everyone. But it was my way of continuing on despite pain—through pain.

Sooner or later, we've got to carry on. Life must go on. The show, the audience, the schedule—all of the people working on the show—those were my responsibilities at the time. Everyone struck with an emotional wallop has commitments to keep. Is it to a job, to a family, or to a higher power? When enduring the unendurable, we can all carry on by plugging into something larger than ourselves.

You are going to mourn, you are going to have pain. But hold tight. Remember, if you reject the difficulty and the scars, the compromises and adaptations that come with age, you are rejecting what has brought you to this moment. Chronic pain becomes a constant companion, I tell myself. Listen to it.

Pain is evidence of consequence. It reminds us that life, for mortals, is a trade-off. We face loss, but we also learn. Becoming mortal, there is something we gain. I think of it as a swap.

The most grounded of us have learned to make use of our pain even when it threatens to subsume us. There are individuals who, facing the most dire circumstances, make it through. Think of Billie Holiday, whose addiction pulled her down, landed her in prison, and nearly killed her career before she launched a comeback. Or Aretha Franklin, who released her first album at age fourteen and pregnant with her second child.

Aretha Franklin was mentored by the great Mahalia Jackson, known as the "Queen of Gospel." Jackson had been born into extreme poverty—she grew up in a three-room house shared with thirteen relatives and a dog. Losing her mother by age five made matters worse. Released into the care of an aunt, she was alternately neglected and abused for the rest of her childhood. But Jackson had been blessed with a priceless voice. Not only did she eventually land a recording contract and become the first gospel singer ever to perform at Carnegie Hall, she used her formidable voice as a force for the civil rights movement.

The depth and power of these women's performances came not just from talent but from living through unimaginable hardship. They sang with what we commonly refer to as "soul." We might also call it gravitas.

"Gravitas" comes from the Latin, *gravis* meaning "heavy." Acquiring this quality means that we become more connected, solid, grounded in wisdom. We are rooted, have our bearings, and it becomes easier to return to a position of stability and strength when there is a disturbance, the proverbial calm in a storm. We become able to handle what life throws our way. While everyone around you panics when your company loses its most lucrative client, or while your family despairs when a beloved matriarch learns she has cancer, or when other parents become manic that there is a lice outbreak at your child's school, your center holds.

Gravitas is one of the better swaps to be made as we sense our loss of immortality. We recognize it in people who have a certain dignity in how they comport themselves. They do not flail about rhetorically or physically; they present a clarity and simplicity in their thinking, movement, and speech. There is a seriousness, a thoughtfulness, seated deep within them. These people have come to a place of peace in dealing with consequence.

Immortals live without consequences. Zeus can go on impregnating mortal girls forever, and his heavenly consort, Hera, will continue to mete out punishment to earthlings for his actions, and Zeus will pay no price. Mortals, however, learn differently.

Throughout his career as a Baptist minister, Martin Luther King, Jr.—an embodiment of gravitas *par excellence*—became more and more familiar with consequence. By the end, his life was under constant surveillance and threat. During his final speech in Birmingham, he presciently acknowledged he might not make it out alive. He had made peace with such a swap.

King was very close with the master of gospel, Mahalia Jackson. At times, feeling discouraged, he would call her and she would sing gospel to him over the phone. She also performed at many of his rallies, including the 1963 March on Washington. Jackson knew her spirituals and she knew how to deliver them. During King's address to the 250,000 people gathered that day, she felt he needed to kick it into high gear, and she yelled to him from fifty feet away in the crowd, "Tell them about the dream, Martin!"

No part of King's planned speech that day included the "I have a dream" segment. But Jackson had heard the dream sermon in Detroit two months earlier, and she could tell this speech in Washington wasn't reaching the audience the way she knew it could. So she called out to him a second time. King then began riffing on this theme and quoting his dream sermon from memory until, after landing finally on "free at last"—a line from a spiritual—he brought one of the great orations in history to a close and, with the help of Mahalia Jackson, the crowd to a fevered pitch.

Gravitas has been an essential quality in leaders since the ancient patriarchs, but politicians and statesmen do not have a monopoly on it. Find it in yourself, in your own way, under the heft of your accumulated experiences. Think of gravitas as the ability to judge. Like King Solomon, you are able to let the extremes burn themselves out and look straight down the middle to find what is right.

The weight of experience is why we are taught to venerate our elders. It's why you're more polite to your grandmother at Thanksgiving than you are with other family members. Trust me, your grandmother knows why you're so nice. But never mind, if you are the grandmother, strong-arm the dinner table. You've earned it. Leverage runs along a spectrum from respect to sympathy to pity, but it's all leverage. While you can remember your past, take credit for having had it. Wise elders know to be glad to give up the imaginary notion that you are immortal in exchange for the very real emotional power of gravitas. If you have it, use it, dammit.

Chapter Ten

Build a Second Act

In the words of Yogi Berra, "When you come to a fork in the road, take it."

President Jimmy Carter, after losing reelection to Ronald Reagan in 1980, suffered the ignominy of a one-term presidency. Some people see his time in office as a failure, others feel his contributions have been overlooked. Regardless, afterward he faced what he then described as "an altogether new, unwanted, and potentially empty life." So he regrouped.

While Carter could have continued as a professional former president, riding out the momentum with speaking gigs and libraries to oversee, he chose instead to take responsibility for his world. Where other presidents leveraged their celebrity or graciously got "out of the way" for their successors, Jimmy Carter created a new template for a post-presidential life and, in doing so, completely reset his reputation and legacy.

He framed his post–White House life by pursuing his pledge to promote peace and health around the globe. He moved his pledge forward by using efficiency, a mastery of what was appropriate for the occasion, and a willingness to clear away what wasn't working.

First, he returned to his peanut farm in Plains, Georgia, and settled his faltering business interests. Then he took time to consider his proudest accomplishment as president—brokering the Camp David accords between Israel and Palestine—and decided to leverage his talent for diplomacy as a private citizen.

Instead of the traditional presidential legacy library, he and his wife, Rosalynn, created the Carter Center as a place to resolve conflicts. He found purpose as a global citizen, narrowing his personal mission to "waging peace" and fighting disease. The story since is well known: the annual work projects for Habitat for Humanity; the dozens of diplomatic missions for succeeding presidents; the high-profile visit to Cuba; the Nobel Peace Prize in 2002; the twenty-eight books that turned him into a forceful, sometimes prickly public intellectual.

Carter blended past and present to do something unprecedented. This was a man who once walked into large rooms with the band playing "Hail to the Chief," yet it was his bounce back from "failed president" to diplomatic humanitarian that allowed him to really achieve gravitas.

Whether nudged into retirement or voluntarily selecting a second act, you, too, must challenge your past. Sometimes what has worked for you in the past outlives its usefulness—just as a workout ceases to yield the benefits it once had. An earned life requires a willingness to look critically at your habits. Identity is hard enough to build once in a lifetime, but to build it time after time requires a radical confrontation with your ego, your limitations, and your changing abilities. You have to be willing to find other ways of being in the world beyond those that have served you well throughout your life. To do this, we must learn, like Carter, to evaluate where we stand in the present, challenging unproductive behaviors.

Techies have a word for any short-term inelegant solution. They call it a *kludge* (it rhymes with "stooge"). The Microsoft Word document on your screen vanishes when it's time to print. Coders write a few lines of code that fixes the matter and allows you to print but does not solve the underlying bug. The code insert is a kludge.

When we are young, often we rush and are tempted to kludge. We come up with a fix and think, "Eh, it's not perfect, but it'll do for now." If you are not careful, as you get older, those quick fixes can become permanently fixed in your ways.

We rely on kludges endlessly in our daily lives, not only with tech crises. Any on-the-spot improvisation to solve a problem qualifies. When you use a paper clip to hold your broken eyeglass frames together, that's a kludge. When you substitute a more convenient ingredient for the costly one the recipe calls for, that's a cooking kludge. When you intentionally close out a tedious explanation by saying "and blah blah blah," that verbal filler is a conversation kludge.

Have you ever done something stupid and pretended it worked? Maybe you agreed to work on a project that was obviously dreck but provided a good paycheck. As you work, you convince yourself it's not so bad, still, it's soul-sucking. You tell yourself next time you'll maintain your integrity and turn it down while you wait for something more stimulating, but then the prospect arises and you figure, what's one more? Before you know it, you're a little richer perhaps, but also miserable.

Examining your past, find the spots where you did something because you needed to adapt (you took that junk gig because you needed the money), but over time the adaptation outlived its usefulness. If you are feeling a twinge of guilt or stupidity with this practice, give up these emotional tongue-lashings and just make the changes.

Your kludges are all the trade-offs and allowances you make to deal with a deflating circumstance—by ignoring, tolerating, or avoiding the situation. Sometimes we're aware that we're settling for less than optimal. Sometimes we believe we don't have any other choice. Like the tax code filling up with loophole after loophole until it is a senseless mess, many kludges are baked into our primary endeavors—to the point where we hardly see them anymore. We treat them as systemic, the way things are. These kludges shackle and slow us down. And they don't autocorrect. Over a lifetime, they remain in force until dekludging reveals a better way. It's possible—even likely—that you're unaware of all the kludges you've relied on in your life.

How do we know we've been kludging? A dead giveaway is that when you describe a kludge to friends they squint at you and go, "Huh?" And you respond with something along the lines of "Oh, yeah, well, that's the way we've always done it," and sort of scurry to move the conversation along.

We can't make perfect choices all the time. But we usually know deep in our bones when we're on a wrong path—and that we should correct the error. You can call on your pledge to determine whether a choice is the right one. Does it strengthen your determination to go for a bigger life or undermine it?

Ask yourself where you rely on autopilot in your life, where you have fallen into a rut. If you were describing your setup to a friend, what part would make you wince and say, "I know, I know, it doesn't make sense, but it works for me." See if you can locate the duct tape you've applied. What would it take to peel it off? What would happen if you did? Would it all fall apart? Is there a solution that would make things stronger in the long run, though it may be difficult in the short term?

Maturity gives us the opportunity to dekludge, and a second act is the perfect time. We've learned that no one else is responsible for our success or survival. It's up to us to erect a stable scaffolding that's not stressed by temporary fixes and what is left can be pretty amazing.

For some, a second act is not an altogether new path but a veer, albeit in the same general direction. These people make exciting, expansive moves, exploring new territory within their field. *Altersstil* (German for "older style") is a term used by art historians to label the late careers of artists who, after a lifetime of committed effort, find a way to relaunch their work into whole new worlds. Works are accomplished that could never have been attempted earlier.

The art historian Meyer Schapiro defined late creativity with the phrase "senile sublime." He used it to refer to work that's liberated from its usual anxiety-producing ambitions. The singing in the shower/dancing in the dark looseness that comes when you unwrap the straps of other people's expectations opens you up to new forms of expression. Think limber, zany, brave, risky, and free, like a great jazz improviser roaming across scales, making leaps, syncopating rhythms, and looping through time with forms repeated but transformed. It is chaos controlled and it is only because these musicians have a bone-deep understanding of how more traditional songs are structured that they can guide what is released into something other than cacophony when that structure is shattered.

This sort of late-in-life artistry not only demonstrates perseverance but reveals one of the great advantages of having time on your side: the opportunity to work with deepening creativity and smarts born of experience. It is only with time that we gain these resources and over time they can become more, not less.

Marcel Proust is the master of retrieving the layers of lost time. His writing uses our sensory capacities—taste, smell, sound—to tease the details of our ancient past from, as he put it, *"L'édifice immense du souvenir"*—"the vast structure of memory"—located deep inside our brains. The famous madeleine dipped in tea floods Proust with memories of his childhood in Combray; walking on uneven Parisian cobblestones returns memories of Venice from years before.

"I stood repeating the movement of a moment, one foot upon the higher flagstone, the other on the lower. This movement caused me joyous certainty. It imposed the past upon the present and made me hesitate as to which time I was existing in. . . . and I enjoyed the existence of time that is outside time."

Thus does Proust describe the effect of rocking. The body moving from heel to toe or from right to left connects him to his deepest memories of the same action in cradle or womb, when indeed time was outside time. The taste of warmth and security and ease—not moving ourselves but being rocked by another—are prelinguistic sensory recollections retained by the memory bank of our muscles. When the same action is repeated over time in different situations, experiences are united through action. As an old man walking in Paris, Proust feels Venice as he knew it decades before as a young man. He recognizes "time outside time" by connecting now to then far back. It is the senile sublime that allows many layers of time to join into one from beginning to end. In the dichotomy-resolving language of *altersstil*, rocking becomes stasis in motion.

ROCKING TO ROLL

Try the following sequence in serenity. Think of nothing but your motion and allow one thing to pass seamlessly into the next as you move from each numbered point to the next.

- Seated on the ground, stretch your legs slightly open out in front of you. Rock gently forward and back evenly. You are keening.

- Lower your forearms between your legs as close to the floor as your back will allow. In this position, rock from side to side.

- Next, lie back flat. Place your right foot on the ground, then lay the left foot on your right knee. Rock right and then left several times. Reverse.

- Now bend your knees and bring your bent legs as close to your chest as possible. We call this the *clamshell.* In this position, rock to your right side. Then return to your back and open the legs, still bent, from the hip. Close the legs and reverse to the left.

- Coordinate your arms. Join your fingers into a steeple and stretch your arms long on your side as you roll right, keeping your hands over your head. You will find you need a bit more momentum to reach the full side stretch. Circle the arms down in front of your chest as you roll to your back, bending your knees up toward your chest in the clamshell. Reverse.

- Now, as you rock to your right, proceed to your stomach by pulling your forearms under your shoulders and also turning your toes under so the metatarsal is pushing into the floor. In this position, rock back onto your shins and into a kneeling position. Next, return to your stomach and reverse your movement through your side to your back. Repeat the series to your left.

- Any time you wish, you can push to your feet from the kneel and continue to a standing position. From there, return through the kneeling position long to your side and then the clamshell as you lie flat on your back again.

This series might seem a bit "new agey," and so it is. It is a variant on the classic yoga movement called the Sun Salutation, and it is close to the movement executed by Hua Chi in Chapter Seven 3,000 times a day. However, it is also the extent of the body's possibilities from stillness to standing. One move evolves organically into the next with no demarcation. Thus rocking becomes rolling and lying flat becomes standing upright. It all circles imperceptibly back from the ending to the beginning, as, assumedly, do we.

Accumulated experiences make us more efficient. In our youth, early efforts can be sprawling, unfurling in multiple directions as we try to establish our best practices. We might require draft after draft of a presentation before landing on the right tone. Knowing when and how to cut to the chase is a skill that can increase rapidly with age.

We learn to live without the extraneous and act more quickly. You knock out that presentation without so much of a grind. For me, because I have decades of choreographing under my belt, a dance that used to take me six weeks to finish now requires three. Hour-long meetings under my control now finish in thirty minutes. I remember what hasn't worked, and I don't call on it very often. Your time is just that—yours. Next time you find a conversation meandering and leeching precious minutes, try to wrap it up with a quick, but polite, "I really must be going now."

Knowing what is appropriate in any particular situation is another tool to use as you build your second act, by which I mean not only what the situation needs but also what works for you. Fred Astaire remains universally admired because he rarely did anything inappropriate—never made a false or ugly dance move, never acted ungenerously with his partners, always dressed impeccably. He could dance with a hat rack in *Royal Wedding* and look good. Astaire—who was dismissed after his first screen test with the memorable, "Can't act. Slightly bald. Can dance a little," exploited every ounce of skill he had (balance, work ethic, uncanny rhythm) and didn't bother with those he didn't have (which is why he rarely strayed from playing the same character in film after film). He possessed an exquisite sense of what was appropriate for him. Did he stiffen as he aged? Yes, he did, but you never noticed because he had already adjusted accordingly.

All master adjusters learn to push their strengths and drop everything else—resentment, insecurity, doubt, physical handicaps.

Beethoven, by the time he wrote his late quartets, had become completely deaf. Yet he managed to coach the Schuppanzigh Quartet, as they prepared to perform his great Opus 132, by watching the motion of their bows and their fingers.

Herman Melville, forgotten almost immediately after the publication of *Moby Dick* (which sold a paltry number of copies in its day), continued writing in private for the next thirty years. During the last five years of his life, he produced *Billy Budd* which, when published posthumously, was declared a masterpiece.

Francisco Goya, deaf and completely isolated from society in his seventies, dove into the black murals of the Quinta del Sordo—a collection revered to this day for its humanity.

Cultural critic Edward Said refers to late works like these as "catastrophes." He liked the idea that older artists could weld irreconcilables together to create entities that didn't seem possible. Auguste Rodin created one of the great sculptural works of the twentieth century by joining two pieces of bronze sculpture, made at vastly different points in his career, to form one memorable, harmonious work, *The Walking Man.*

The Walking Man started in 1877 with a sculpture of Saint John the Baptist preaching, a full figure standing midstride on muscled legs open like a compass. Some ten years later, Rodin worked separately on an armless torso, inspired by the drawings of Michelangelo. Ten years after that, at the peak of his career—the 1890s—he decided to reuse the legs from Saint John the Baptist and slapped his unfinished torso right on top. These two works have different proportions, are sculpted from different angles, and have absolutely no connection to one another.

And yet Rodin had the smarts and the audacity to stick one on top of the other—no need for a transition. He joins the two and says, "Buy it." It's fragmented, unfinished, and it looks pretty great. Who knew? He conveys power and drive with an armless, headless, storyless figure that represents a bold and crucial step into modern art.

The Walking Man is not just brilliant, it is also humorous with the wit of serendipity. Surely Rodin looked at it with a grin when he first saw it completed. With age, we are able to get away with the outrageous, the unreasonable, the impossible. With so much experience to choose from, we can select unexpected combinations that provide a jolt of mischievous glee. In that moment you realize that even just by being alive, you are cheating time and getting away with bloody murder.

We also develop a bemused patience with the obstacles in our life. They become old friends. You encounter your bump, and rather than be tripped up by it again, you think, "You've got to be kidding. You again?" Instead of feeling frustration and shame, you feel amused and prepare to force it into service.

Giuseppe Verdi had been composing for over fifty years—and yet, toward the end of his life, he thought he wanted to write another opera. He had finished twenty-seven, what was one more? But nearing ninety, he was unsure of himself, full of doubt that he would be able to complete the work at his age. Bitch, bitch, moan, moan. Enter Arrigo Boito. The two had worked together earlier on another opera, and when Boito heard that Verdi was privately considering one more, off Boito went to work—also in private—on a libretto using the story of Shakespeare's Falstaff, a comic, cowardly knight.

Several months later, Boito presented Verdi with *Falstaff* whole. So Verdi set aside his doubts and began. He was in good health and through a long career, had cultivated the stamina to continue composing. He decided,

Build a Second Act

"Amen; so be it! So let's do *Falstaff*! For now, let's not think of obstacles, of age, of illnesses!" His decision was made: let's get on with it. Let's do it.

Remarkably, he turned the last act into a fugue—a funny fugue. Definitely a first in operatic history. We think of fugues as dense exercises in solemnity, but when he came up with this notion, Verdi is reported to have said, audaciously, "After having relentlessly massacred so many heroes and heroines, I have at last the right to laugh a little." What he accomplished should have been impossible, but like Rodin and his *Walking Man*, Verdi saw conjunctions that would never have occurred to him as a younger man. He was able to make something absurdly sublime with his boffo fugue.

At the end of this opera, following a massive swell—in fact a huge swell as Verdi was a master orchestrator—Falstaff, himself a fat, failed fool who always manages to prevail, proclaims to the cast and to the audience in a whisper, "He who laughs last laughs best." So two (as they might have said of themselves) old fucks—Falstaff and Verdi—overcome the odds to triumph in this final challenge.

D on't give up on yourself. Your identity is never a done deal. It is always a work in progress. Think back to our friend Hokusai taking up a new name over and over, his identity shifting but his pledge unwavering. Hokusai wrote, "From the age of six, I had a passion for copying the form of things and since the age of fifty I have published many drawings, yet of all I drew by my seventieth year there is nothing worth taking into account. At seventy-three years I partly understood the structure of animals, birds, insects and fishes, and the life of grasses and plants. And so, at eighty-six I shall progress further; at ninety I shall even further penetrate their secret meaning, and by one hundred I shall perhaps truly have reached the level of the marvelous and divine. When I am one hundred and ten, each dot, each line will possess a life of its own."

Know your intentions. Trust to your pledge. Get on with your second act. A third could be waiting.

Chapter Eleven

Stronger for the Mending

Exercise 11: Master of the Mundane *Page 163*

Imagine waking up with an intense shock of pain behind your eye. It's upsetting, disorienting, but you continue on with your preparations for the day—or you try. It turns out you cannot control your limbs. Your left side goes numb, and when you try to speak, the sounds are unrecognizable as words. You are transported, it seems, outside your physical body, able to watch yourself from afar as you attempt to shower. It is unlike any experience you have ever had, which is disturbing, and yet even as you struggle to make sense of what is happening, you are overcome with an otherworldly degree of attention to your surroundings, hyperconscious of each atom, each molecule. You find yourself overcome with a state of euphoria. This is not a communication from the divine. You are having a stroke.

Jill Bolte Taylor had always been fascinated by the workings of our brains. Her early curiosity was sparked by questions about how her brother's schizophrenic brain differed from her own. She became a neuroanatomist, studying—and later teaching—at Harvard. Through her research, she developed as good an idea as anyone about what goes on in our two hemispheres. Her nuanced understanding of neurology gave her extraordinary insight into what was happening inside her own skull when she suffered a massive hemorrhage in her brain at just thirty-seven.

More than simply painful, some events in our lives are so significant that they are life-changing, seismic shifts that are as serious as it gets, and the course of the rest of our days can depend on how we respond.

From the moment her brain "went offline," as Taylor puts it in her book, *My Stroke of Insight*, she was transported to a state of childlike innocence and ignorance. With the help of her mother and her doctors, she painstakingly relearned everything from what tuna salad is to how to walk and read and think again, but her reacquaintance with the physical world was accompanied by a new sense of being at one with the universe. She was acutely aware of herself as made up of fluid within a membrane, able to move and change. She had to let go of the person she had been. When she lost the ability to do things without thinking—even simple things, like walking—she learned to put more of her energy into just being.

Taylor knew precisely what was going on at a neurological level—how her cerebellum was affected, which neurological pathways were compromised, etc.—which makes it all the more surprising that, as she worked over the next decade to recover, to get back the faculties she'd lost, she also found herself trying to recall her initial state of euphoria, to hold on to it. Taylor's transformation after the hemorrhage in her brain went beyond learning to walk and speak again. She found herself utterly changed. As she put it, "I morphed from feeling small to feeling enormous and expansive."

Taylor claimed responsibility for her own recovery. No one was going to take those exhausting steps to the bathroom for her. She would do it herself, on her terms, measuring success by her own standards, not by those, even, to which she had adhered for over a decade as a brain researcher. Best practices in neurology, for example, said that any skills she had not recovered by six months after the incident would remain out of reach, but she spent eight years slowly working her way back. As she writes, "The try is everything."

You can either look at change as a betrayal of your world's order or, like Taylor, use your challenges and try to develop a broader perspective.

This moment came for me when I required a major surgery. Six years of working around the metatarsal I had broken earlier in Atlanta resulted in a badly deteriorated hip socket. Until then, dancing, no matter how difficult or physically demanding, had always been a sacred trust, the fulfillment of my pledge to respect and work hard with what I had, surgery-free. But now my body was telling me that the more I worked, the worse it got. I felt out of control and this became a constant preoccupation. I began to sense myself a failure and this in turn was ballooning into my identity.

Being no longer able to trust myself was new territory and I had little hope for my prospects post-surgery. I felt certain I would not be able to regain the strength or range of motion I had before. Having delayed all such intervention up until age seventy-six, this for me represented a defeat, a verification of mortality from which there was no going back. I was literally wearing out.

Filled with doubt, I scheduled the surgery. The doctors deemed it a success. Now the physical pain was gone, but I had to acknowledge that the pact between me and my limbs had been broken.

Still, as I began healing following the surgery, I found my priority more focused than it had been in a very long time, as I no longer sought to compensate for pain. I had one mission and one mission only: to recover. Not working became healing. That was the job.

But as I rested in my apartment, I was still uncertain and confused. It was back to basics for me. I had to relearn how to stand. I worked to improve my posture daily—summoning the very old-fashioned and ever relevant image of balancing a book on my head as I walked—and slowly I felt dignity returning. Presence comes with posture.

Bit by small bit, I gradually developed a better perspective than when I went into the surgery. I found that being hobbled seemed a lot better than being dead. I felt grateful to be alive, albeit in a more vulnerable shell. "Barn's burnt down—now I can see the moon," the haiku by the seventeenth-century Japanese poet Mizuta Masahide exercises this feeling. In other words, when something we have relied upon for years falls away, what else is revealed to us that we couldn't see before? My take? Once you realize the scope of the loss, don't just stand there staring at the moon, build a new barn.

And while you are at it, include a moon-viewing platform.

You must choose whether you will retreat or surge forward after you are shattered by your version of physical betrayal and redefinition. For example, the dissolution of a long marriage might send you scurrying home into solitude, or it might be a chance to spend time with new people who will bring an influx of new ideas, activities, and emotions into your life if you welcome them. Or say you've had to take a new job after you've been let go; you could play it safe in the new gig to try to ensure job security, or you could view a new location and job as a clean slate ready to have a more exciting story written upon it. As ever, the choice rests with you: expand or contract.

Remember our old nemesis, status quo bias? The fear of making the wrong choice can be powerful, dissuading us from taking risks. As I was recovering, I did not venture outside for a month. I claimed it was because the ground was uneven, the weather too cold, but really, I knew it was because I did not want to be seen with a cane and limping. My comfortable space was condensed to the walls around my apartment. The frame for the choices I was making was one of uncertainty, and it kept me caged in. I entered a no-man's-land where I was hung up between who I had been and who I would become.

When you are shut down by uncertainty and brought low, ask yourself—when was the last time you felt truly ashamed of trying? Was it as bad as you feared it would be? By contrast, when was the last time you felt ashamed of not trying? I'd wager that sting was worse.

Bit by bit, things were allowed to just become what they would be, and by the sixth month following the surgery, I began to take great solace in small known things. There is nourishment in routine, blessed routine, to be found like a cactus finds water in the desert air. Perfection was just a fantasy existing in someone else's mind. My routine became a sanctuary for me. I enjoyed regularity, the mundane, not because they were pedestrian but because I was awakened to their pleasures as if I were a child experiencing them for the first time. Foremost of all these pleasures was walking.

I found myself thinking of Thoreau's essay "Walking." As I took some of my first fawnlike steps, I thought of his suggestion that it is only when you are ready to lay aside all that you've accumulated, your many experiences, demands, failures, that you are ready, truly, to walk. Wobbly on my feet, I heard Thoreau's words, "We find it difficult to choose our direction, because it does not yet exist distinctly in our idea." Ah, yes. Intention. I moved because I had a goal—recovery—and it animated my muscles and my grit. I thought, too, of how Thoreau seemed to derive sustenance, vigor from wildness he encountered while walking through the so untamed, unpredictable, risky. There is value there. It was not learning about walking as I had walked before. It was about learning to walk. I started to feel whole. I might not have been dancing but I was walking, and I thought, simply, *Is this not amazing?*

Bear this in mind as you recover from whatever has brought you down: grant yourself some grace. As I balanced on one leg, the other swinging round through a very wide center, I would urge my leg to get closer to a straight line on the next try, putting one foot in front of the next. It was tremendously simple and tremendously difficult all at once. I found that nothing could be taken for granted. But I tried to be nice about it. At least it was a small positive step in the right direction, for the body hates negativity—"not" is outside its vocabulary.

Each day my body got a little better, remembered its business; found it actually did still know how to walk and then, later, bike, sidestep, and touch its toe forward, side, and back. One muscle at a time, I tightened and stretched and found myself determined to get back into the physical fray, asking nonverbal questions of space and time of the sort that only movement can reveal. And remember.

I have a cell phone video of the very first steps my grandson took. He is, of course, beautiful, amazing, and reminds me every time how incredibly courageous we all are as little mites lurching about in space. Going back to the beginning and learning to walk again is a daunting task to be sure, but what freedom to be able to learn something for the second time, being able to draw on the lessons you learned the first time around.

Finally, as muscle memory started to kick in, I began to recognize myself. My present could recall its past. The room took a larger shape as I felt its dimensions again. I expanded my steps outward, eventually putting on a little music. I could not help myself—I did not even realize I was dancing until I was. Either I tricked myself or I forgot to be pissed off. The dancing was nothing radical, but rhythmic, expressive. Improvement suddenly seemed possible and I became brave again.

One of the best things that happened as I recovered was rereading Montaigne. The only thing more remarkable than the words he used is how he came to write them. Having retired as a magistrate in sixteenth-century France, he needed to recalibrate big-time to reidentify his purpose and renew his existence, so he holed up in his library where he created a new genre, the essay. Rather than interacting in high-powered diplomatic positions, he held a mirror to human experience illuminating how we pass our time routinely, tackling everyday subjects—friendship, cruelty, wearing clothes, and also why we cry and laugh at the same thing sometimes. He never presumed to have a final answer. His favorite line was drenched in skepticism: "What do I know?" Montaigne was a one-off, an original, of course. But his example can instruct and inspire us as we stare down the challenge of continuing a rich life, pondering the pressing but mundane question, "What do I do now?"

Like Montaigne, we might profit from a careful examination of the mundane. In painting, it is the masters of still life—Corot, Rembrandt, van Eyck, Vermeer—who could paint the illusion of fruits, vegetables, and fish that would make you want to pluck them from the frame, who are the keepers of the quotidian. Theirs was an extraordinary skill—called *trompe l'oeil* or "fool the eye"—that allowed them to make an illusion into reality. Finding absolute beauty in the humble, the everyday, the living, the growing, the becoming is a skill that can be practiced with more than just the eye.

After her stroke, Jill Bolte Taylor found that she was exquisitely tuned in to her surroundings, to people's body language and facial expressions. As astonishing as her physical comeback was, what transformed Taylor was the way her life expanded after the stroke to include the sense of euphoria she had first felt during the hemorrhage. The stroke was no longer an obstacle in her life but rather simply an event. She found a deep sense of conviction that "peace is only a thought away." She felt she was able to attain it through a deep focus on the here and now, as she relished food, the texture of her clothing, and the feeling of hair draping on her shoulders.

I, too, found myself overcome by an appreciation for small things as I recovered from my injury—the intense pleasure of turning an avocado in my hand, the absolute triumph in feeling the sun on my neck, a marvelous glimpse of the moon in the evening sky. For about the millionth time I decided to start learning to cook. Amazed and awed to be alive, the quotidian became my comfort zone.

MASTER OF THE MUNDANE

By definition, we overlook the mundane in our lives—the workaday struts that hold us up and the surroundings that provide the backdrop to the drama of our lives. And thank God. Imagine attending to every turn of a faucet, every nick in the floorboard, or every gust of wind. It would be like trying to have a conversation in the middle ring of a circus. Too much. And yet selectively turning the beam of your attention on the quotidian can provoke and inspire.

Even breathing must sometimes be relearned for pain, like stress, confuses our natural rhythms. Remember it is in on the preparation, out on the work. Seated, feel your body prepare an action as you inhale—say, moving your hand toward a cup—and then on the exhale do the work and move the cup. Again.

Or try this.

Go to a museum and find a painting of the most commonplace subject you can imagine—a still life of a pitcher on a table, a valley, a single house. Ask yourself what the artist saw in this subject that made it feel worthy of capturing on canvas. Can inhabiting the mind of the artist help you to see what is glorious about this everyday object?

Now think of a time when your routine was disrupted—perhaps moving house required you to learn again where to find the flour in your pantry or a dry cleaner you could trust. What felt invigorating to relearn and what felt comforting to settle into anew? Can you find one small part of your life to undo and start over fresh? Unpack your silverware drawer and reorganize it as if for the first time. Find a new salutation or closing for your emails. Sit in a different seat at the conference table. What kind of impact does this have on your thinking?

> Finally, know that your disasters are themselves but mundane things. Having a great surgeon insert a new hip socket is far less severe than finding yourself alone in the shower with heart failure. Perspective always reduces our misfortunes to more manageable proportions.

So often we refer to people who have recovered from disaster as "fighters," but I think this is the wrong tack. Fighting is acknowledging that you might lose or might not perform to someone else's standards. I prefer to think of life as a pursuit, constantly chasing, never quite reaching your ideal . . . and learning to get over it.

We must be clear: attaining perfection as you recover is never the goal because it is, of course, impossible. Deadlines are too short. Bodies won't cooperate. Colleagues are not fully committed. Perfectionism is the ultimate waste of time because you're pursuing the nonexistent. I once asked a businessman about his ideal day. "No such thing," he said. "You have good days and bad, and occasionally, something unprecedented happens. But you never have the perfect number of customers, or cash flow, or new products in the wings. Your day rarely unfolds exactly as you planned it. Your talks with employees are never understood perfectly. This applies to everything."

In my early years, I wouldn't have understood his answer. I believed that I could match the idealized picture in my head with what I did onstage if I worked harder. Time helps you realize you never arrive at perfection. You're perpetually approaching it. That's the best we can do—and that's okay.

Listen to what life is telling you. Are you stronger than you think? Or is whatever you are defining as a betrayal really telling you that control is an illusion? And finally, can you turn this into an opportunity for you to improve upon things?

While I was at it, I figured I might as well not just "get well" but also raise the bar. In coming back, I gave myself a new sort of challenge: work on my old bugaboo, balance. My balance has always sucked, and so I wondered, could I not just recover what I had, but also improve upon it?

As I came back to walking, I applied myself to this bigger goal, enhancing my balance. I toiled with the therapist to be steadier, and I was grateful that I could not just get better but that I could get *better*.

And all over again, I had an awakened sense of how lucky we are when we are able to recover. My recovery reminded me of the practice of *kintsugi*—gold mending. This is to take a damaged vessel and patch it with gold, exemplifying the principle of *wabi-sabi*, the idea of embracing the flawed, the imperfect. The perfect porcelain is vulnerable as it awaits disaster. The patched porcelain knows how to handle vicissitudes. When we can heal, we are stronger for the mending. Once you have been denied something, reacquiring it is a gift unto itself. As the saying goes, you don't miss the water till the well runs dry. We learn to give thanks.

Chapter Twelve

Shut Up and Dance

Exercise 12: Mentoring for All *Page 175*

W e are all dancers.

Too often civilians view dancing as something for the chosen few, only the elite who can command their bodies to move with extreme precision and grace. Many people see dance as an impenetrable fortress, but no, there is no temple with high priests guarding the gates. In reality, some of the greatest dancers are amateurs—those who do it for love, not professional gain.

I can't tell you how often audience members approach me after a show and begin their praise with "I don't know anything about dance, but . . ." "Nonsense," I say. "Are you walking? Are you moving through time and space? Then you are dancing."

Dance, in its many forms—tap, ballroom, street, boogying in your bedroom—belongs to everyone. Pioneers of modern dance broke with the rigorous tradition of ballet and forged a different way—not *the* way, a way. Find your own. You do not need experts to show you the way in. You can walk, sit, stand, maybe even run. Take it from there.

Wake up and dance, y'all. As you best see fit. Dancing is a beautiful way to say thank you to your body and to join the human race. Welcome to the tribe.

I wrote this book to enlarge my tribe, by sharing with you examples of people who have continued to dance throughout their lives, who have stuck with a pledge to move and expand instead of shrink and contract, and have reaped the rewards. In this moment, one of my personal favorites is marathoner Eliud Kipchoge—twenty-six seconds away from breaking the two-hour mark.

As a youngster in Kenya, Kipchoge came from an area where he had to walk for miles just to get to school. His father died before he ever saw his son. Kipchoge was running barefoot, training himself in a virtual void for seventeen years, and then finding a trainer to help him pursue excellence.

It is his discipline, his intelligence, his faith in the limitless possibilities of the human body that I find beautiful. I find beauty, too, in the wedge formation he has made a group of runners trained to time the distance and also break the wind by running in front of him. Seven runners plus Kipchoge with one goal, one cadence. That kind of solidarity, of shared purpose, gives me hope.

It is both physically and psychologically more difficult to run alone, it is also necessary at some point. Kipchoge ran the last half of his record-breaking Berlin marathon solo. Having just taken more than a minute off the world record, he crossed the finish line with his trademark focus and calm intact. Kipchoge ran with the same form at the beginning as when he finished the race. Beauty.

I admire, too, Kipchoge saying that he was not simply going for the record but for his personal best. This hits home for dancers.

Dance has no goals, so dancers never develop the narrow focus of a stopwatch or a perfect score, or any outside metric to tell you whether you have done what you set out to do or not. As a dancer, you are always pushing for your optimal performance, competing only with yourself. There is no opposing team. With no other way to measure your success, it is only ever, *Have I done my personal best?* Wise words for dance and the rest of your life. Was it your best show or not? Was it part of your pledge? If not, what can you improve? In this spirit, the only winner is you.

Olympic gold medal–winning figure skater John Curry lived by this philosophy. He was expert at completing his school figures, crisp, clean 8's and 0's carved on the ice. These were graded—it was simple to tell if you were off by even a fraction of an inch. The ice told the story. In competition, judges evaluated power, how many turns completed in the air, but John didn't go for that. He was an artist, and he wanted to dance, not simply compete, on ice. He was hungry for the challenge of what dance brings: invention, variety, creativity. He knew each show had to be his personal best.

I do not skate, but when John asked me to make a solo for him I stood by the rink in Madison Square Garden at four in the morning—the only time we could get ice—as he skated his impeccable school figures to warm up. Demanding but utterly gorgeous. Watching in this silent white space it was as if time didn't exist. Past, present, and what came next—all were gone in the cold air as John repeated the figures over and over. The space became a sanctuary.

As we were working, I questioned everything. He naturally turned to the right; sometimes I had him turn left. He skated mostly clockwise. I sent him the other way. Both of these adjustments required him to break with his muscle memory. Not easy. But he did not run from the challenge, he relished it. This took him out of his comfort zone where the ice was predictable, into a state of discovery.

With John's control, his transfers of weight from one blade to the next were invisible. This suggested to me the notion of asking him to circle the periphery of the rink balanced on one leg, pushing off just once and then gliding to a stop precisely where he had begun at the center of the massive rink. It was as if he had stopped time.

Time is slippery. It is like water—transforming from something solid as ice to something as fleeting as vapor. It can go from being invisible to impenetrable, and the transition is imperceptible. I often think I am not dancing in space but rather in an ongoing flow of time.

As a choreographer, I witness the fluidity of time as I work with my regisseurs. These are my most trusted people, the instructors who train the next generation of dancers to take care of my work and present it to the world. I treat them as disciples (joking that Christ needed twelve, and one of those turned out to be a dud, so I better get thirty—or more!—ready).

My dances are like my children, and these disciples are like my designated caretakers to ensure the dances will thrive. Dance has yet to come up with a better way of passing along a piece than reconstructing it in living performances, which creates an inescapable tension. On the one hand, dance is fleeting, ephemeral, lasting only as long as the moments when bodies cross the stage. The curtain falls. The end. On the other hand, while architecture, paintings, and texts can be chipped, burned, flooded, stolen, or lost, a dance can be reconstructed indefinitely into the future, as long as there are willing bodies to project the movement. Dance's ephemerality becomes its biggest virtue. Each dance must be seen in real time and danced by real people, taught by other real people.

Right now, as I write, there are four regisseurs—Sara, Shelley, Susan, Stacey—spread across the country, preparing dances to go up. All have danced with me for over two decades. I made original work for them, shared thousands of hours of studio time with them.

Today I work with them differently. They are all over sixty and now occupy center stage differently. They become trustees of the dance for they are teaching. It is on them to communicate with our young dancers so that these new performances can radiate truth and positivity, instead of seeming confused about their purpose.

It is no small challenge to present a dance years after its premiere. How do you connect with an audience who, reminiscent of our Dylan cult, wants the same show exactly as it was thirty years ago? It's an impossible ask. These are different dancers, different bodies, and a radically different context—different leaders, different wars, different planet. So when we enter the studio now to revisit a dance from our common past, I inquire with my regisseurs, *What is still relevant, what still lives?*

At the end of the day, my goal is to know that when I am not here anymore to look over their shoulder, I won't be able to bitch, looking down from up there, because I had my shot and I will have used it well. Ultimately, this means I must surrender my position as master. This is how we leave our mark; we access something that refuses to die and pass it along. It is also how we continue to learn, by going from novice to master and then recognizing when we have no more to teach.

This happens in the Zen monastery when the novice apprentices himself to a master. The novice continually fails to live up to the standards and receives firm correction for his lapses of attention, his jumpy, untrained monkey mind, as the master applies the *keisaku*, or "enlightenment stick." Yes, there is pain, but as the novice adjusts his thinking, integrating other perspectives into his mind-set, he becomes an active participant in his own education. Finally, at the end of the novice's lessons, the master bows and, with the last of his blows, says, "Go find yourself another master. I have nothing more to teach you."

Both parties benefit, because when the novice arrives with his genuine curiosity, he brings freshness to the master and the master while passing on his knowledge, draws energy from the novice. Theirs is not strictly a mentorship but a kind of collaboration, which is how I see my relationship with my regisseurs. In the ritual of speaking the words "I have nothing more to teach you," the master reveals his humility, his frank acceptance of his limitations, and his acknowledgment that no one can know everything. Thus the final lesson of the master: when you can let yourself off the hook for knowing it all, there is freedom.

My good friend the author Maurice Sendak envied my exposure to dancers who were twenty to forty years my junior. It is a privilege that comes with the choreographer's job, no different than a schoolteacher being surrounded by young people. Maurice appreciated the irony that he was one of the world's most celebrated children's book authors and yet, with no children of his own, he spent nearly all his time either alone in his studio or in the company of adults. He loved to come into rehearsals. His envy, I suspect, didn't spring from some deep need to pass on wisdom to a younger generation but, rather, the other way around: he desired what younger people could teach him.

MENTORING FOR ALL

It's all too easy to be ghettoized with people your own age, agreeing on things like snow was colder in our day, roads longer. We're as tribal about age as we are about class, race, and political persuasion. It's a cycle that needs to be broken.

Here's an exercise in visiting a younger tribe. Identify younger acquaintances you admire or respect. Age and relationship are irrelevant. The key is that these people have done something in the past that impressed you—meaning they have something valuable to share. Whatever it is—a technical skill or a passion for music or an obsession with playing bridge—ask them to teach you what they know. I doubt you'll get much resistance.

Beware the temptation to slip into the role of master. Relax into the mind of the novice. There you will almost always have the wiggle room to expand your thinking.

> We learn best when we can forget ourselves. That is when we can respect our teachers and do what they say without running their thinking through our judgmental process. Dancers, too, learn best by following behind others. Watch how a friend walks and literally put yourself in their shoes. Study their gait, notice the size of their step, feel their rhythm as they shift their weight. Are there eccentricities through the hip and are these mannerisms or necessity? From this exercise compassion will follow.

Maurice had the mind of a child big-time. A great walker, he roamed the hundreds of acres of land he'd accumulated over thirty years. Accompanied by a walking stick and Max, his German shepherd, he walked every day for the last twenty years of his life. He ritualized his search for the new in his daily constitutional. I knew him to allot at least an hour to find just one novel color or form, one discovery, each day. He wanted to find what hadn't been seen and harvest it to use in his work.

He found inspiration in art as well as nature. On the days I joined him for his walks, we would come back to sit at the breakfast table and take out one of his treasures. Maurice was a collector of things bought mostly at auction. Original Turners, Blakes, Rembrandt etchings, Lewis Carroll photographs. Mozart letters. Keats's death mask. These we could hold, touch, smell, breathe. Our fingers grazed the same spot that Mozart's had centuries ago. It was electric, like actually becoming the great man himself, if only for a moment. The transfer of energy felt quite literal. Handing over one of the pale pages, I felt the child's physical fragility in Mozart's letter to his mother, written from tour as a small boy, sending her in a postscript one million kisses. Maurice considered the greatest tribute to his own work to be word from the mother of a five-year-old who had written to Maurice requesting a signature, and then promptly eaten the paper Maurice had sent.

For Maurice, childhood was not something to be outgrown. He had a special relationship to the young, not simply because they were his readers—in fact, he despised the "kiddie book author" moniker so often attached to his name—but because he knew powerfully the feeling of waiting to be discovered, like a child eagerly performing a trick for someone's approval. Though he was not received publicly as a sophisticate, Maurice, at heart, wanted people to know he was writing about the human condition, not just life as a childhood lark, and he took solace in the company of his favorite overlooked greats: Melville dying forgotten until *Billy Budd* revived his reputation, Schubert's penniless young death, Blake's near-anonymity at his.

I visited Maurice a few weeks before he died at his home in Connecticut. When it was time for me to leave, he walked me to the car. He was frail, relying on two canes to get around, which could be a nerve-racking prospect when the ground was icy as it was that day. As I rolled down the window to wave goodbye, he lifted one of the canes high in the air, anchored himself with the other, and executed a nifty little jig for my amusement.

Here was a guy of eighty-three, using his low center of gravity, digging in, pushing with a great deal of effort to balance on one leg on ice, dancing wildly away. In life you can shuffle along carefully, or you can dance. Even on ice. The choice is yours.

With his dance, Maurice did not say goodbye with language, he said it in dance, in movement. That is life. Movement is life, dance is life.

Even the greatest master of words, William Shakespeare, knew the power of ending with dance. After his plays were performed at the Globe, he brought the performance to a close with dance. Once the last words had sorted out the chaos of the play's story, but before the crowd could leave, he returned the audience to the real world—not artifice but life itself. The players unmasked themselves, the music started, and the cast danced. Shakespeare knew when it was time to shut up and dance.

Here is a dancer's pledge. It is like a string tied around your finger reminding you to keep it moving.

PLEDGE TO MOVE

- I will set aside a few moments each day when, though the past is slippery, there are no debts owed and I can be free.

- I will look then for my community, for those who carry themselves with awareness, who know their space and, grateful for their time, have asked the questions that go beyond ego.

- Taking hands we shall circle wide, laying our shoulders back and letting the light bathe our faces as we move in a single whirling mass.

- Then we can open our circle to flow concentrically inward until it spirals, revolving from forward to backward and inside to outside.

- There the beginning is the end and the end the beginning.

- And so we dance.

Thanks

Thanks to Simon & Schuster editor Karyn Marcus, who allowed for movement to be the equivalent of language between the covers of a book, and continued to think, long past sanity, that this could be a good book. Jon Karp, S&S publisher who listened to her; the S&S sales force—Cary Goldstein, Julia Prosser, Elizabeth Breeden—who helped me insist that you need this book. Also Becky Cole, who helped me figure out why I didn't want to write the book in the first place, and Molly Gregory, who sleuthed out what the blue butterflies that kept appearing in my manuscript were. Then too, David Rosenthal and Mark Reiter, who finished *The Creative Habit* and started this one off, and Andrew Wylie, who has managed to survive me for a very long time now. Also to Laura Shapiro who showed me how exceedingly smart Shakespeare actually was.